Balaustion's Adventure by Robert Browning

Including A Transcript From Euripides

"Our Euripides, the Human,
With his droppings of warm tears,
And his touches of things common
Till they rose to touch the spheres."

Robert Browning is one of the most significant Victorian Poets and, of course, English Poetry.

Much of his reputation is based upon his mastery of the dramatic monologue although his talents encompassed verse plays and even a well-regarded essay on Shelley during a long and prolific career.

He was born on May 7th, 1812 in Walmouth, London. Much of his education was home based and Browning was an eclectic and studious student, learning several languages and much else across a myriad of subjects, interests and passions.

Browning's early career began promisingly. The fragment from his intended long poem Pauline brought him to the attention of Dante Gabriel Rossetti, and was followed by Paracelsus, which was praised by both William Wordsworth and Charles Dickens. In 1840 the difficult Sordello, which was seen as willfully obscure, brought his career almost to a standstill.

Despite these artistic and professional difficulties his personal life was about to become immensely fulfilling. He began a relationship with, and then married, the older and better known Elizabeth Barrett. This new foundation served to energise his writings, his life and his career.

During their time in Italy they both wrote much of their best work. With her untimely death in 1861 he returned to London and thereafter began several further major projects.

The collection Dramatis Personae (1864) and the book-length epic poem The Ring and the Book (1868-69) were published and well received; his reputation as a venerated English poet now assured.

Robert Browning died in Venice on December 12th, 1889.

Index of Contents

If I mention the simple truth, that this poem absolutely owes its existence to you,—who not only suggested, but imposed on me as a task, what has proved the most delightful of May-month amusements,—I shall seem honest, indeed, but hardly prudent; for, how good and beautiful ought such a poem to be!

Euripides might fear little; but I, also, have an interest in the performance; and what wonder if I beg you to suffer that it make, in another and far easier sense, its nearest possible approach to those Greek qualities of goodness and beauty, by laying itself gratefully at your feet?

R. B.
LONDON, July 23, 1871.

NOTE

After the publication of the fourth volume of The Ring and the Book in February, 1869, Browning published nothing until March, 1871, when he printed Hervé Riel in the Cornhill Magazine, afterward including it in his first new volume of collected poems. In August of the same year appeared the first of his larger ventures in the field of Greek life. This poem was followed four years later by Aristophanes' Apology, and it is so intimately connected with Balaustion's Adventure that in this edition it is made to follow it, though the chronological sequence was broken, as will be seen, by the composition and publication of other considerable works. The motto at the head of the poem is from Mrs. Browning, and in the last lines of the poem Browning couples her with his friend Sir Frederick Leighton.

BALUSTION'S ADVENTURE

About that strangest, saddest, sweetest song
I, when a girl, heard in Kameiros once,
And, after, saved my life by? Oh, so glad
To tell you the adventure!
        Petalé,
Phullis, Charopé, Chrusion! You must know,
This "after" fell in that unhappy time
When poor reluctant Nikias, pushed by fate,
Went falteringly against Syracuse;
And there shamed Athens, lost her ships and men,
And gained a grave, or death without a grave.
I was at Rhodes—the isle, not Rhodes the town,
Mine was Kameiros—when the news arrived:
Our people rose in tumult, cried, "No more
Duty to Athens, let us join the League
And side-with Sparta, share the spoil,—at worst,
Abjure a headship that will ruin Greece!"
And so, they sent to Knidos for a fleet

To come and help revolters. Ere help came,—
Girl as I was, and never out of Rhodes
The whole of my first fourteen years of life,
But nourished with Ilissian mother's-milk,—
I passionately cried to who would hear
And those who loved me at Kameiros—"No!
Never throw Athens off for Sparta's sake—
Never disloyal to the life and light
Of the whole world worth calling world at all!
Rather go die at Athens, lie outstretched
For feet to trample on, before the gate
Of Diomedes or the Hippadai,
Before the temples and among the tombs,
Than tolerate the grim felicity
Of harsh Lakonia! Ours the fasts and feasts,
Choës and Chutroi; ours the sacred grove,
Agora, Dikasteria, Poikilé,
Pnux, Keramikos; Salamis in sight,
Psuttalia, Marathon itself, not far!
Ours the great Dionusiac theatre,
And tragic triad of immortal fames,
Aischulos, Sophokles, Euripides!
To Athens, all of us that have a soul,
Follow me!" And I wrought so with my prayer,
That certain of my kinsfolk crossed the strait
And found a ship at Kaunos; well-disposed
Because the Captain—where did he draw breath
First but within Psuttalia? Thither fled
A few like-minded as ourselves. We turned
The glad prow westward, soon were out at sea,
Pushing, brave ship with the vermilion cheek,
Proud for our heart's true harbor. But a wind
Lay ambushed by Point Malea of bad fame,
And leapt out, bent us from our course. Next day
Broke stormless, so broke next blue day and next.
"But whither bound in this white waste?" we plagued
The pilot's old experience: "Cos or Crete?"
Because he promised us the land ahead.
While we strained eyes to share in what he saw,
The Captain's shout startled us; round we rushed:
What hung behind us but a pirate-ship
Panting for the good prize! "Row! harder row!
Row for dear life!" the Captain cried: "'t is Crete,
Friendly Crete looming large there! Beat this craft
That 's but a keles, one-benched pirate-bark,
Lokrian, or that bad breed off Thessaly!
Only, so cruel are such water-thieves,
No man of you, no woman, child, or slave,

But falls their prey, once let them board our boat!"
So, furiously our oarsmen rowed and rowed:
And when the oars nagged somewhat, dash and dip,
As we approached the coast and safety, so
That we could hear behind us plain the threats
And curses of the pirate panting up
In one more throe and passion of pursuit,—
Seeing our oars flag in the rise and fall,
I sprang upon the altar by the mast
And sang aloft—some genius prompting me—
That song of ours which saved at Salamis:
"O sons of Greeks, go, set your country free,
Free your wives, free your children, free the fanes
O' the Gods, your fathers founded,—sepulchres
They sleep in! Or save all, or all be lost!"
Then, in a frenzy, so the noble oars
Churned the black water white, that well away
We drew, soon saw land rise, saw hills grow up,
Saw spread itself a sea-wide town with towers,
Not fifty stadia distant; and, betwixt
A large bay and a small, the islet-bar,
Even Ortugia's self—oh, luckless we!
For here was Sicily and Syracuse:
We ran upon the lion from the wolf.
Ere we drew breath, took counsel, out there came
A galley, hailed us. "Who asks entry here
In war-time? Are you Sparta's friend or foe?"
"Kaunians,"—our Captain judged his best reply,
"The mainland-seaport that belongs to Rhodes;
Rhodes that casts in her lot now with the League,
Forsaking Athens,—you have heard belike!"
"Ay, but we heard all Athens in one ode
Just now! we heard her in that Aischulos!
You bring a boatful of Athenians here,
Kaunians although you be: and prudence bids,
For Kaunos' sake, why, carry them unhurt
To Kaunos, if you will: for Athens' sake,
Back must you, though ten pirates blocked the bay!
We want no colony from Athens here,
With memories of Salamis, forsooth,
To spirit up our captives, that pale crowd
I' the quarry, whom the daily pint of corn
Keeps in good order and submissiveness."
Then the gray Captain prayed them by the Gods,
And by their own knees, and their fathers' beards,
They should not wickedly thrust suppliants back,
But save the innocent on traffic bound—
Or, maybe, some Athenian family

Perishing of desire to die at home,—
From that vile foe still lying on its oars,
Waiting the issue in the distance. Vain!
Words to the wind! And we were just about
To turn and face the foe, as some tired bird
Barbarians pelt at, drive with shouts away
From shelter in what rocks, however rude,
She makes for, to escape the kindled eye,
Split beak, crook'd claw o' the creature, cormorant
Or ossifrage, that, hardly baffled, hangs
Afloat i' the foam, to take her if she turn.
So were we at destruction's very edge,
When those o' the galley, as they had discussed
A point, a question raised by somebody,
A matter mooted in a moment,—"Wait!"
Cried they (and wait we did, you may be sure).
"That song was veritable Aischulos,
Familiar to the mouth of man and boy,
Old glory: how about Euripides?
The newer and not yet so famous bard,
He that was born upon the battle-day
While that song and the salpinx sounded him
Into the world, first sound, at Salamis—
Might you know any of his verses too?"

Now, some one of the Gods inspired this speech:
Since ourselves knew what happened but last year—
How, when Gulippos gained his victory
Over poor Nikias, poor Demosthenes,
And Syracuse condemned the conquered force
To dig and starve i' the quarry, branded them—
Freeborn Athenians, brute-like in the front
With horse-head brands,—ah, "Region of the Steed"!—
Of all these men immersed in misery,
It was found none had been advantaged so
By aught in the past life he used to prize
And pride himself concerning,—no rich man
By riches, no wise man by wisdom, no
Wiser man still (as who loved more the Muse)
By storing, at brain's edge and tip of tongue,
Old glory, great plays that had long ago
Made themselves wings to fly about the world,—
Not one such man was helped so at his need
As certain few that (wisest they of all)
Had, at first summons, oped heart, flung door wide
At the new knocking of Euripides,
Nor drawn the bolt with who cried "Decadence!
And, after Sophokles, be nature dumb!"

Such,—and I see in it God Bacchos' boon
To souls that recognized his latest child,
He who himself, born latest of the Gods,
Was stoutly held impostor by mankind,—
Such were in safety: any who could speak
A chorus to the end, or prologize,
Roll out a rhesis, wield some golden length
Stiffened by wisdom out into a line,
Or thrust and parry in bright monostich,
Teaching Euripides to Syracuse—
Any such happy man had prompt reward:
If he lay bleeding on the battlefield
They stanched his wounds and gave him drink and food;
If he were slave i' the house, for reverence
They rose up, bowed to who proved master now,
And bade him go free, thank Euripides!
Ay, and such did so: many such, he said,
Returning home to Athens, sought him out,
The old bard in the solitary house,
And thanked him ere they went to sacrifice.
I say, we knew that story of last year!

Therefore, at mention of Euripides,
The Captain crowed out, "Euoi, praise the God!
Oöp, boys, bring our owl-shield to the fore!
Out with our Sacred Anchor! Here she stands,
Balaustion! Strangers, greet the lyric girl!
Euripides! Babai! what a word there 'scaped
Your teeth's enclosure, quoth my grandsire's song!
Why, fast as snow in Thrace, the voyage through,
Has she been falling thick in flakes of him!
Frequent as figs at Kaunos, Kaunians said.
Balaustion, stand forth and confirm my speech!
Now it was some whole passion of a play;
Now, peradventure, but a honey-drop
That slipt its comb i' the chorus. If there rose
A star, before I could determine steer
Southward or northward—if a cloud surprised
Heaven, ere I fairly hollaed 'Furl the sail!'—
She had at fingers' end both cloud and star;
Some thought that perched there, tame and tunable,
Fitted with wings; and still, as off it flew,
'So sang Euripides,' she said, 'so sang
The meteoric poet of air and sea,
Planets and the pale populace of heaven,
The mind of man, and all that 's made to soar!'
And so, although she has some other name,
We only call her Wild-pomegranate-flower,

Balaustion; since, where'er the red bloom burns
I' the dull dark verdure of the bounteous tree,
Dethroning, in the Rosy Isle, the rose,
You shall find food, drink, odor, all at once;
Cool leaves to bind about an aching brow,
And, never much away, the nightingale.
Sing them a strophe, with the turn-again,
Down to the verse that ends all, proverb-like,
And save us, thou Balaustion, bless the name!"

But I cried, "Brother Greek! better than so,—
Save us, and I have courage to recite
The main of a whole play from first to last;
That strangest, saddest, sweetest song of his,
ALKESTIS; which was taught, long years ago
At Athens, in Glaukinos' archonship,
But only this year reached our Isle o' the Rose.
I saw it at Kameiros; played the same,
They say, as for the right Lenean feast
In Athens; and beside the perfect piece—
Its beauty and the way it makes you weep,—
There is much honor done your own loved God
Herakles, whom you house i' the city here
Nobly, the Temple wide Greece talks about!
I come a suppliant to your Herakles!
Take me and put me on his temple-steps,
To tell you his achievement as I may,
And, that told, he shall bid you set us free!"

Then, because Greeks are Greeks, and hearts are hearts,
And poetry is power,—they all outbroke
In a great joyous laughter with much love:
"Thank Herakles for the good holiday!
Make for the harbor! Row, and let voice ring,
'In we row, bringing more Euripides!'"
All the crowd, as they lined the harbor now,
"More of Euripides!"—took up the cry.
We landed; the whole city, soon astir,
Came rushing out of gates in common joy
To the suburb temple; there they stationed me
O' the topmost step: and plain I told the play,
Just as I saw it; what the actors said,
And what I saw, or thought I saw the while,
At our Kameiros theatre, clean-scooped
Out of a hillside, with the sky above
And sea before our seats in marble row:
Told it, and, two days more, repeated it,
Until they sent us on our way again

With good words and great wishes.
                      Oh, for me—
A wealthy Syracusan brought a whole
Talent and bade me take it for myself:
I left it on the tripod in the fane,
—For had not Herakles a second time
Wrestled with Death and saved devoted ones?—
Thank-offering to the hero. And a band
Of captives, whom their lords grew kinder to
Because they called the poet countryman,
Sent me a crown of wild-pomegranate-flower:
So, I shall live and die Balaustion now.
But one—one man—one youth,—three days, each day,—
(If, ere I lifted up my voice to speak,
I gave a downward glance by accident,)
Was found at foot o' the temple. When we sailed,
There, in the ship too, was he found as well,
Having a hunger to see Athens too.
We reached Peiraieus; when I landed—lo,
He was beside me. Anthesterion-month
Is just commencing: when its moon rounds full,
We are to marry. O Euripides!
I saw the master: when we found ourselves
(Because the young man needs must follow me)
Firm on Peiraieus, I demanded first
Whither to go and find him. Would you think?
The story how he saved us made some smile:
They wondered strangers were exorbitant
In estimation of Euripides.
He was not Aischulos nor Sophokles:
—"Then, of our younger bards who boast the bay,
Had I sought Agathon, or Iophon,
Or, what now had it been Kephisophon?
A man that never kept good company,
The most unsociable of poet-kind,
All beard that was not freckle in his face!"

I soon was at the tragic house, and saw
The master, held the sacred hand of him
And laid it to my lips. Men love him not:
How should they? Nor do they much love his friend
Sokrates: but those two have fellowship:
Sokrates often comes to hear him read,
And never misses if he teach a piece.
Both, being old, will soon have company,
Sit with their peers above the talk. Meantime,
He lives as should a statue in its niche;
Cold walls enclose him, mostly darkness there,

Alone, unless some foreigner uncouth
Breaks in, sits, stares an hour, and so departs,
Brain-stuffed with something to sustain his life,
Dry to the marrow 'mid much merchandise.
How should such know and love the man?
                        Why, mark!
Even when I told the play and got the praise,
There spoke up a brisk little somebody,
Critic and whippersnapper, in a rage
To set things right: "The girl departs from truth!
Pretends she saw what was not to be seen,
Making the mask of the actor move, forsooth!
'Then a fear flitted o'er the wife's white face,'—
'Then frowned the father,'—'then the husband shook,'—
'Then from the festal forehead slipt each spray,
And the heroic mouth's gay grace was gone;'—
As she had seen each naked fleshly face,
And not the merely-painted mask it wore!"
Well, is the explanation difficult?
What 's poetry except a power that makes?
And, speaking to one sense, inspires the rest,
Pressing them all into its service; so
That who sees painting, seems to hear as well
The speech that 's proper for the painted mouth;
And who hears music, feels his solitude
Peopled at once—for how count heartbeats plain
Unless a company, with hearts which beat,
Come close to the musician, seen or no?
And who receives true verse at eye or ear,
Takes in (with verse) time, place, and person too,
So, links each sense on to its sister-sense,
Grace-like: and what if but one sense of three
Front you at once? The sidelong pair conceive
Through faintest touch of finest finger-tips,—
Hear, see and feel, in faith's simplicity,
Alike, what one was sole recipient of:
Who hears the poem, therefore, sees the play.
Enough and too much! Hear the play itself!
Under the grape-vines, by the streamlet-side,
Close to Baccheion; till the cool increase,
And other stars steal on the evening-star,
And so, we homeward flock i' the dusk, we five!
You will expect, no one of all the words
O' the play but is grown part now of my soul,
Since the adventure. 'T is the poet speaks:
But if I, too, should try and speak at times,
Leading your love to where my love, perchance,
Climbed earlier, found a nest before you knew—

Why, bear with the poor climber, for love's sake!
Look at Baccheion's beauty opposite,
The temple with the pillars at the porch!
See you not something beside masonry?
What if my words wind in and out the stone
As yonder ivy, the God's parasite?
Though they leap all the way the pillar leads,
Festoon about the marble, foot to frieze,
And serpentiningly enrich the roof,
Toy with some few bees and a bird or two,—
What then? The column holds the cornice up!

There slept a silent palace in the sun,
With plains adjacent and Thessalian peace—
Pherai, where King Admetos ruled the land.

Out from the portico there gleamed a God,
Apollon: for the bow was in his hand,
The quiver at his shoulder, all his shape
One dreadful beauty. And he hailed the house,
As if he knew it well and loved it much:
"O Admeteian domes, where I endured,
Even the God I am, to drudge awhile,
Do righteous penance for a reckless deed,
Accepting the slaves' table thankfully!"
Then told how Zeus had been the cause of all,
Raising the wrath in him which took revenge
And slew those forgers of the thunderbolt
Wherewith Zeus blazed the life from out the breast
Of Phoibos' son Asklepios (I surmise,
Because he brought the dead to life again),
And so, for punishment, must needs go slave,
God as he was, with a mere mortal lord:
—Told how he came to King Admetos' land,
And played the ministrant, was herdsman there,
Warding all harm away from him and his
Till now; "For, holy as I am," said he,
"The lord I chanced upon was holy too:
Whence I deceived the Moirai, drew from death
My master, this same son of Pheres,—ay,
The Goddesses conceded him escape
From Hades, when the fated day should fall,
Could he exchange lives, find some friendly one
Ready, for his sake, to content the grave.
But trying all in turn, the friendly list,
Why, he found no one, none who loved so much,
Nor father, nor the aged mother's self

That bore him, no, not any save his wife,
Willing to die instead of him and watch
Never a sunrise nor a sunset more:
And she is even now within the house,
Upborne by pitying hands, the feeble frame
Gasping its last of life out; since to-day
Destiny is accomplished, and she dies,
And I, lest here pollution light on me,
Leave, as ye witness, all my wonted joy
In this dear dwelling. Ay,—for here comes Death
Close on us of a sudden! who, pale priest
Of the mute people, means to bear his prey
To the house of Hades. The symmetric step!
How he treads true to time and place and thing,
Dogging day, hour and minute, for death's-due!"

And we observed another Deity,
Half in, half out the portal,—watch and ward,—
Eying his fellow: formidably fixed,
Yet faltering too at who affronted him,
As somehow disadvantaged, should they strive.
Like some dread heapy blackness, ruffled wing,
Convulsed and cowering head that is all eye,
Which proves a ruined eagle who, too blind
Swooping in quest o' the quarry, fawn or kid,
Descried deep down the chasm 'twixt rock and rock,
Has wedged and mortised, into either wall
O' the mountain, the pent earthquake of his power;
So lies, half hurtless yet still terrible,
Just when—who stalks up, who stands front to front,
But the great lion-guarder of the gorge,
Lord of the ground, a stationed glory there!
Yet he too pauses ere he try the worst
O' the frightful unfamiliar nature, new
To the chasm, indeed, but elsewhere known enough,
Among the shadows and the silences
Above i' the sky: so, each antagonist
Silently faced his fellow and forbore.
Till Death shrilled, hard and quick, in spite and fear:

"Ha, ha, and what mayst thou do at the domes,
Why hauntest here, thou Phoibos? Here again
At the old injustice, limiting our rights,
Balking of honor due us Gods o' the grave?
Was 't not enough for thee to have delayed
Death from Admetos,—with thy crafty art
Cheating the very Fates,—but thou must arm
The bow-hand and take station, press 'twixt me

And Pelias' daughter, who then saved her spouse,—
Did just that, now thou comest to undo,—
Taking his place to die, Alkestis here?"

But the God sighed, "Have courage! All my arms,
This time, are simple justice and fair words."

Then each plied each with rapid interchange:

"What need of bow, were justice arms enough?"

"Ever it is my wont to bear the bow."

"Ay, and with bow, not justice, help this house!"

"I help it, since a friend's woe weighs me too."

"And now,—wilt force from me this second corpse?"

"By force I took no corpse at first from thee."

"How then is he above ground, not beneath?"

"He gave his wife instead of him, thy prey."

"And prey, this time at least, I bear below!"

"Go take her!—for I doubt persuading thee ..."

"To kill the doomed one? What my function else?"

"No! Rather, to dispatch the true mature."

"Truly I take thy meaning, see thy drift!"

"Is there a way then she may reach old age?"

"No way! I glad me in my honors too!"

"But, young or old, thou tak'st one life, no more!"

"Younger, they die, greater my praise redounds!"

"If she die old,—the sumptuous funeral!"

"Thou layest down a law the rich would like."

"How so? Did wit lurk there and 'scape thy sense?"

"Who could buy substitutes would die old men."

"It seems thou wilt not grant me, then, this grace?"

"This grace I will not grant: thou know'st my ways."

"Ways harsh to men, hateful to Gods, at least!"

"All things thou canst not have: my rights for me!"

And then Apollon prophesied,—I think,
More to himself than to impatient Death,
Who did not hear or would not heed the while,—
For he went on to say, "Yet even so,
Cruel above the measure, thou shalt clutch
No life here! Such a man do I perceive
Advancing to the house of Pheres now,
Sent by Eurustheus to bring out of Thrace,
The winter world, a chariot with its steeds!
He indeed, when Admetos proves the host,
And he the guest, at the house here,—he it is
Shall bring to bear such force, and from thy hands
Rescue this woman! Grace no whit to me
Will that prove, since thou dost thy deed the same,
And earnest too my hate, and all for naught!"

But how should Death or stay or understand?
Doubtless, he only felt the hour was come,
And the sword free; for he but flung some taunt—
"Having talked much, thou wilt not gain the more!
This woman, then, descends to Hades' hall
Now that I rush on her, begin the rites
O' the sword; for sacred, to us Gods below,
That head whose hair this sword shall sanctify!"

And, in the fire-flash of the appalling sword,
The uprush and the outburst, the onslaught
Of Death's portentous passage through the door,
Apollon stood a pitying moment-space:
I caught one last gold gaze upon the night
Nearing the world now: and the God was gone,
And mortals left to deal with misery,
As in came stealing slow, now this, now that
Old sojourner throughout the country-side,
Servants grown friends to those unhappy here:
And, cloudlike in their increase, all these griefs
Broke and began the over-brimming wail,

Out of a common impulse, word by word.

"What now may mean the silence at the door?
Why is Admetos' mansion stricken dumb?
Not one friend near, to say if we should mourn
Our mistress dead, or if Alkestis lives
And sees the light still, Pelias' child—to me,
To all, conspicuously the best of wives
That ever was toward husband in this world!
Hears any one or wail beneath the roof,
Or hands that strike each other, or the groan
Announcing all is done and naught to dread?
Still not a servant stationed at the gates!
O Paian, that thou wouldst dispart the wave
O' the woe, be present! Yet, had woe o'erwhelmed
The housemates, they were hardly silent thus:
It cannot be, the dead is forth and gone.
Whence comes thy gleam of hope? I dare not hope:
What is the circumstance that heartens thee?
How could Admetos have dismissed a wife
So worthy, unescorted to the grave?
Before the gates I see no hallowed vase
Of fountain-water, such as suits death's door;
Nor any clipt locks strew the vestibule,
Though surely these drop when we grieve the dead,
Nor hand sounds smitten against youthful hand,
The women's way. And yet—the appointed time—
How speak the word?—this day is even the day
Ordained her for departing from its light.
O touch calamitous to heart and soul!
Needs must one, when the good are tortured so,
Sorrow,—one reckoned faithful from the first."

Then their souls rose together, and one sigh
Went up in cadence from the common mouth:
How "Vainly—anywhither in the world
Directing or land-labor or sea-search—
To Lukia or the sand-waste, Ammon's seat—
Might you set free their hapless lady's soul
From the abrupt Fate's footstep instant now.
Not a sheep-sacrificer at the hearths
Of Gods had they to go to: one there was
Who, if his eyes saw light still,—Phoibos' son,—
Had wrought so, she might leave the shadowy place
And Hades' portal: for he propped up Death's
Subdued ones, till the Zeus-flung thunder-flame
Struck him; and now what hope of life were hailed
With open arms? For, all the king could do

Is done already,—not one God whereof
The altar fails to reek with sacrifice:
And for assuagement of these evils—naught!"

But here they broke off, for a matron moved
Forth from the house: and, as her tears flowed fast,
They gathered round. "What fortune shall we hear?
For mourning thus, if aught affect thy lord,
We pardon thee: but lives the lady yet
Or has she perished?—that we fain would know!"

"Call her dead, call her living, each style serves,"
The matron said: "though grave-ward bowed, she breathed;
Nor knew her husband what the misery meant
Before he felt it: hope of life was none:
The appointed day pressed hard; the funeral pomp
He had prepared too."
                    When the friends broke out,
"Let her in dying know herself at least
Sole wife, of all the wives 'neath the sun wide,
For glory and for goodness!"—"Ah, how else
Than best? who controverts the claim?" quoth she:
"What kind of creature should the woman prove
That has surpassed Alkestis?—surelier shown
Preference for her husband to herself
Than by determining to die for him?
But so much all our city knows indeed:
Hear what she did indoors and wonder then!
For, when she felt the crowning day was come,
She washed with river-waters her white skin,
And, taking from the cedar closets forth
Vesture and ornament, bedecked herself
Nobly, and stood before the hearth, and prayed:
'Mistress, because I now depart the world,
Falling before thee the last time, I ask—
Be mother to my orphans! wed the one
To a kind wife, and make the other's mate
Some princely person: nor, as I who bore
My children perish, suffer that they too
Die all untimely, but live, happy pair,
Their full glad life out in the fatherland!'
And every altar through Admetos' house
She visited and crowned and prayed before,
Stripping the myrtle-foliage from the boughs,
Without a tear, without a groan,—no change
At all to that skin's nature, fair to see,
Caused by the imminent evil. But this done,—
Reaching her chamber, falling on her bed,

There, truly, burst she into tears and spoke:
'O bride-bed, where I loosened from my life
Virginity for that same husband's sake
Because of whom I die now—fare thee well!
Since nowise do I hate thee: me alone
Hast thou destroyed; for, shrinking to betray
Thee and my spouse, I die: but thee, O bed,
Some other woman shall possess as wife—
Truer, no! but of better fortune, say!'
—So falls on, kisses it till all the couch
Is moistened with the eyes' sad overflow.
But when of many tears she had her fill,
She flings from off the couch, goes headlong forth,
Yet—forth the chamber—still keeps turning back
And casts her on the couch again once more.
Her children, clinging to their mother's robe,
Wept meanwhile: but she took them in her arms,
And, as a dying woman might, embraced
Now one and now the other: 'neath the roof,
All of the household servants wept as well,
Moved to compassion for their mistress; she
Extended her right hand to all and each,
And there was no one of such low degree
She spoke not to nor had an answer from.
Such are the evils in Admetos' house.
Dying,—why, he had died; but, living, gains
Such grief as this he never will forget!"

And when they questioned of Admetos, "Well—
Holding his dear wife in his hands, he weeps;
Entreats her not to give him up, and seeks
The impossible, in fine: for there she wastes
And withers by disease, abandoned now,
A mere dead weight upon her husband's arm.
Yet, none the less, although she breathe so faint,
Her will is to behold the beams o' the sun:
Since never more again, but this last once,
Shall she see sun, its circlet or its ray.
But I will go, announce your presence,—friends
Indeed; since 't is not all so love their lords
As seek them in misfortune, kind the same:
But you are the old friends I recognize."

And at the word she turned again to go:
The while they waited, taking up the plaint
To Zeus again: "What passage from this strait?
What loosing of the heavy fortune fast
About the palace? Will such help appear,

Or must we clip the locks and cast around
Each form already the black peplos' fold?
Clearly the black robe, clearly! All the same,
Pray to the Gods!—like Gods' no power so great!
O thou king Paian, find some way to save!
Reveal it, yea, reveal it! Since of old
Thou found'st a cure, why, now again become
Releaser from the bonds of Death, we beg,
And give the sanguinary Hades pause!"
So the song dwindled into a mere moan,
How dear the wife, and what her husband's woe;
When suddenly—
                    "Behold, behold!" breaks forth:
"Here is she coming from the house indeed!
Her husband comes, too! Cry aloud, lament,
Pheraian land, this best of women, bound—
So is she withered by disease away—
For realms below and their infernal king!
Never will we affirm there's more of joy
Than grief in marriage; making estimate
Both from old sorrows anciently observed,
And this misfortune of the king we see—
Admetos who, of bravest spouse bereaved,
Will live life's remnant out, no life at all!"

So wailed they, while a sad procession wound
Slow from the innermost o' the palace, stopped
At the extreme verge of the platform-front:
There opened, and disclosed Alkestis' self,
The consecrated lady, borne to look
Her last—and let the living look their last—
She at the sun, we at Alkestis.
                    We!
For would you note a memorable thing?
We grew to see in that severe regard,—
Hear in that hard dry pressure to the point,
Word slow pursuing word in monotone,—
What Death meant when he called her consecrate
Henceforth to Hades. I believe, the sword—
Its office was to cut the soul at once
From life,—from something in this world which hides
Truth, and hides falsehood, and so lets us live
Somehow. Suppose a rider furls a cloak
About a horse's head; unfrightened, so,
Between the menace of a flame, between
Solicitation of the pasturage,
Untempted equally, he goes his gait
To journey's end: then pluck the pharos off!

Show what delusions steadied him i' the straight
O' the path, made grass seem fire and fire seem grass,
All through a little bandage o'er the eyes!
As certainly with eyes unbandaged now
Alkestis looked upon the action here,
Self-immolation for Admetos' sake;
Saw, with a new sense, all her death would do,
And which of her survivors had the right,
And which the less right, to survive thereby.
For, you shall note, she uttered no one word
Of love more to her husband, though he wept
Plenteously, waxed importunate in prayer—
Folly's old fashion when its seed bears fruit.
I think she judged that she had bought the ware
O' the seller at its value,—nor praised him
Nor blamed herself, but, with indifferent eye,
Saw him purse money up, prepare to leave
The buyer with a solitary bale—
True purple—but in place of all that coin,
Had made a hundred others happy too,
If so willed fate or fortune! What remained
To give away, should rather go to these
Than one with coin to clink and contemplate.
Admetos had his share and might depart,
The rest was for her children and herself.
(Charopé makes a face: but wait awhile!)
She saw things plain as Gods do: by one stroke
O' the sword that rends the life-long veil away.
(Also Euripedes saw plain enough:
But you and I, Charopé!—you and I
Will trust his sight until our own grow clear.)

"Sun, and thou light of day, and heavenly dance
O' the fleet cloud—figure!" (so her passion paused,
While the awe-stricken husband made his moan,
Muttered now this now that ineptitude:
"Sun that sees thee and me, a suffering pair,
Who did the Gods no wrong whence thou shouldst die!")
Then, as if caught up, carried in their course,
Fleeting and free as cloud and sunbeam are,
She missed no happiness that lay beneath:
"O thou wide earth, from these my palace roofs,
To distant nuptial chambers once my own
In that Iolkos of my ancestry!"—
There the flight failed her. "Raise thee, wretched one!
Give us not up! Pray pity from the Gods!"

Vainly Admetos: for "I see it—see

The two-oared boat! The ferryer of the dead,
Charon, hand hard upon the boatman's-pole,
Calls me—even now calls—'Why delayest thou?
Quick! Thou obstructest all made ready here
For prompt departure: quick, then!'"
                              "Woe is me!
A bitter voyage this to undergo,
Even i' the telling! Adverse Powers above,
How do ye plague us!"
                    Then a shiver ran:
"He has me—seest not?—hales me,—who is it?—
To the hall o' the Dead—ah, who but Hades' self,
He, with the wings there, glares at me, one gaze
All that blue brilliance, under the eyebrow!
What wilt thou do? Unhand me! Such a way
I have to traverse, all unhappy one!"

"Way—piteous to thy friends, but, most of all,
Me and thy children: ours assuredly
A common partnership in grief like this!"

Whereat they closed about her; but "Let be!
Leave, let me lie now! Strength forsakes my feet.
Hades is here, and shadowy on my eyes
Comes the night creeping. Children—children, now
Indeed, a mother is no more for you!
Farewell, O children, long enjoy the light!"

"Ah me, the melancholy word I hear,
Oppressive beyond every kind of death!
No, by the Deities, take heart nor dare
To give me up—no, by our children too
Made orphans of! But rise, be resolute,
Since, thou departed, I no more remain!
For in thee are we bound up, to exist
Or cease to be—so we adore thy love!"

—Which brought out truth to judgment. At this word
And protestation, all the truth in her
Claimed to assert itself: she waved away
The blue-eyed black-wing'd phantom, held in check
The advancing pageantry of Hades there,
And, with no change in her own countenance,
She fixed her eyes on the protesting man,
And let her lips unlock their sentence,—so!

"Admetos,—how things go with me thou seest,—
I wish to tell thee, ere I die, what things

I will should follow. I—to honor thee,
Secure for thee, by my own soul's exchange,
Continued looking on the daylight here—
Die for thee—yet, if so I pleased, might live,
Nay, wed what man of Thessaly I would,
And dwell i' the dome with pomp and queenliness.
I would not,—would not live bereft of thee,
With children orphaned, neither shrank at all,
Though having gifts of youth wherein I joyed.
Yet, who begot thee and who gave thee birth,
Both of these gave thee up; no less, a term
Of life was reached when death became them well,
Ay, well—to save their child and glorious die:
Since thou wast all they had, nor hope remained
Of having other children in thy place.
So, I and thou had lived out our full time,
Nor thou, left lonely of thy wife, wouldst groan
With children reared in orphanage: but thus
Some God disposed things, willed they so should be.
Be they so! Now do thou remember this,
Do me in turn a favor—favor, since
Certainly I shall never claim my due,
For nothing is more precious than a life:
But a fit favor, as thyself wilt say,
Loving our children here no less than I,
If head and heart be sound in thee at least.
Uphold them, make them masters of my house,
Nor wed and give a step-dame to the pair,
Who, being a worse wife than I, through spite
Will raise her hand against both thine and mine.
Never do this at least, I pray to thee!
For hostile the new-comer, the step-dame,
To the old brood—a very viper she
For gentleness! Here stand they, boy and girl;
The boy has got a father, a defence
Tower-like, he speaks to and has answer from:
But thou, my girl, how will thy virginhood
Conclude itself in marriage fittingly?
Upon what sort of sire-found yoke-fellow
Art thou to chance? with all to apprehend—
Lest, casting oh thee some unkind report,
She blast thy nuptials in the bloom of youth.
For neither shall thy mother watch thee wed,
Nor hearten thee in childbirth, standing by
Just when a mother's presence helps the most!
No, for I have to die: and this my ill
Comes to me, nor to-morrow, no, nor yet
The third day of the month, but now, even now,

I shall be reckoned among those no more.
Farewell, be happy! And to thee, indeed,
Husband, the boast remains permissible
Thou hadst a wife was worthy! and to you,
Children; as good a mother gave you birth."

"Have courage!" interposed the friends. "For him
I have no scruple to declare—all this
Will he perform, except he fail of sense."

"All this shall be—shall be!" Admetos sobbed:
"Fear not! And, since I had thee living, dead
Alone wilt thou be called my wife: no fear
That some Thessalian ever styles herself
Bride, hails this man for husband in thy place!
No woman, be she of such lofty line
Or such surpassing beauty otherwise!
Enough of children: gain from these I have,
Such only may the Gods grant! since in thee
Absolute is our loss, where all was gain.
And I shall bear for thee no year-long grief,
But grief that lasts while my own days last, love!
Love! For my hate is she who bore me, now:
And him I hate, my father: loving-ones
Truly, in word not deed! But thou didst pay
All dearest to thee down, and buy my life,
Saving me so! Is there not cause enough
That I who part with such companionship
In thee, should make my moan? I moan, and more:
For I will end the feastings—social flow
O' the wine friends flock for, garlands and the Muse
That graced my dwelling. Never now for me
To touch the lyre, to lift my soul in song
At summons of the Lydian flute; since thou
From out my life hast emptied all the joy!
And this thy body, in thy likeness wrought
By some wise hand of the artificers,
Shall lie disposed within my marriage-bed:
This I will fall on, this enfold about,
Call by thy name,—my dear wife in my arms
Even though I have not, I shall seem to have—
A cold delight, indeed, but all the same
So should I lighten of its weight my soul!
And, wandering my way in dreams perchance,
Thyself wilt bless me: for, come when they will,
Even by night our loves are sweet to see.
But were the tongue and tune of Orpheus mine,
So that to Koré crying, or her lord,

In hymns, from Hades I might rescue thee—
Down would I go, and neither Plouton's dog
Nor Charon, he whose oar sends souls across,
Should stay me till again I made thee stand
Living, within the light! But, failing this,
There, where thou art, await me when I die,
Make ready our abode, my housemate still!
For in the selfsame cedar, me with thee
Will I provide that these our friends shall place,
My side lay close by thy side! Never, corpse
Although I be, would I division bear
From thee, my faithful one of all the world!"

So he stood sobbing: nowise insincere,
But somehow child-like, like his children, like
Childishness the world over. What was new
In this announcement that his wife must die?
What particle of pain beyond the pact
He made, with eyes wide open, long ago—
Made and was, if not glad, content to make?
Now that the sorrow, he had called for, came,
He sorrowed to the height: none heard him say,
However, what would seem so pertinent,
"To keep this pact, I find surpass my power:
Rescind it, Moirai! Give me back her life,
And take the life I kept by base exchange!
Or, failing that, here stands your laughing-stock
Fooled by you, worthy just the fate o' the fool
Who makes a pother to escape the best
And gain the worst you wiser Powers allot!"
No, not one word of this: nor did his wife
Despite the sobbing, and the silence soon
To follow, judge so much was in his thought—
Fancy that, should the Moirai acquiesce,
He would relinquish life nor let her die.
The man was like some merchant who, in storm,
Throws the freight over to redeem the ship:
No question, saving both were better still.
As it was,—why, he sorrowed, which sufficed.
So, all she seemed to notice in his speech
Was what concerned her children. Children, too,
Bear the grief and accept the sacrifice.
Rightly rules nature: does the blossomed bough
O' the grape-vine, or the dry grape's self, bleed wine?

So, bending to her children all her love,
She fastened on their father's only word
To purpose now, and followed it with this:

"O children, now yourselves have heard these things—
Your father saying he will never wed
Another woman to be over you,
Nor yet dishonor me!"

        "And now at least
I say it, and I will accomplish too!"

"Then, for such promise of accomplishment,
Take from my hand these children!"

        "Thus I take—
Dear gift from the dear hand!"

        "Do thou become
Mother, now, to these children in my place!"

"Great the necessity, I should be so,
At least, to these bereaved of thee!"

        "Child—child!
Just when I needed most to live, below
Am I departing from you both!"

        "Ah me!
And what shall I do, then, left lonely thus?"

"Time will appease thee: who is dead is naught."

"Take me with thee—take, by the Gods below!"

"We are sufficient, we who die for thee."

"O Powers, ye widow me of what a wife!"

"And truly the dimmed eye draws earthward now!"

"Wife, if thou leav'st me, I am lost indeed!"

"She once was—now is nothing, thou mayst say."

"Raise thy face, nor forsake thy children thus!"

"Ah, willingly indeed I leave them not!
But—fare ye well, my children!"

        "Look on them—
Look!"

"I am nothingness."

      "What dost thou? Leav'st ..."

"Farewell!"

     And in the breath she passed away.
"Undone—me miserable!" moaned the king,
While friends released the long-suspended sigh.
"Gone is she: no wife for Admetos more!"

Such was the signal: how the woe broke forth,
Why tell?—or how the children's tears ran fast
Bidding their father note the eyelids' stare,
Hands' droop, each dreadful circumstance of death.

"Ay, she hears not, she sees not: I and you,
'T is plain, are stricken hard and have to bear!"
Was all Admetos answered; for, I judge,
He only now began to taste the truth:
The thing done lay revealed, which undone thing,
Rehearsed for fact by fancy, at the best,
Never can equal. He had used himself
This long while (as he muttered presently)
To practise with the terms, the blow involved
By the bargain, sharp to bear, but bearable
Because of plain advantage at the end.
Now that, in fact not fancy, the blow fell—
Needs must he busy him with the surprise.
"Alkestis—not to see her nor be seen,
Hear nor be heard of by her, any more
To-day, to-morrow, to the end of time—
Did I mean this should buy my life?" thought he.

So, friends came round him, took him by the hand,
Bade him remember our mortality,
Its due, its doom: how neither was he first,
Nor would be last, to thus deplore the loved.

"I understand," slow the words came at last.
"Nor of a sudden did the evil here
Fly on me: I have known it long ago,
Ay, and essayed myself in misery;
Nothing is new. You have to stay, you friends,
Because the next need is to carry forth
The corpse here: you must stay and do your part,
Chant proper pæan to the God below;

Drink-sacrifice he likes not. I decree
That all Thessalians over whom I rule
Hold grief in common with me; let them shear
Their locks, and be the peplos black they show!
And you who to the chariot yoke your steeds,
Or manage steeds one-frontleted,—I charge,
Clip from each neck with steel the mane away!
And through my city, nor of flute nor lyre
Be there a sound till twelve full moons succeed.
For I shall never bury any corpse
Dearer than this to me, nor better friend:
One worthy of all honor from me, since
Me she has died for, she and she alone."

With that, he sought the inmost of the house,
He and his dead, to get grave's garniture,
While the friends sang the pæan that should peal.
"Daughter of Pelias, with farewell from me,
I' the house of Hades have thy unsunned home!
Let Hades know, the dark-haired deity,—
And he who sits to row and steer alike,
Old corpse-conductor, let him know he bears
Over the Acherontian lake, this time,
I' the two-oared boat, the best—oh, best by far
Of womankind! For thee, Alkestis Queen!
Many a time those haunters of the Muse
Shall sing thee to the seven-stringed mountain-shell,
And glorify in hymns that need no harp,
At Sparta when the cycle comes about,
And that Karneian month wherein the moon
Rises and never sets the whole night through:
So too at splendid and magnificent
Athenai. Such the spread of thy renown,
And such the lay that, dying, thou hast left
Singer and sayer. Oh that I availed
Of my own might to send thee once again
From Hades' hall, Kokutos' stream, by help
O' the oar that dips the river, back to-day!"
So, the song sank to prattle in her praise:
"Light, from above thee, lady, fall the earth,
Thou only one of womankind to die,
Wife for her husband! If Admetos take
Anything to him like a second spouse—
Hate from his offspring and from us shall be
His portion, let the king assure himself!
No mind his mother had to hide in earth
Her body for her son's sake, nor his sire
Had heart to save whom he begot,—not they,

The white-haired wretches! only thou it was,
I' the bloom of youth, didst save him and so die!
Might it be mine to chance on such a mate
And partner! For there 's penury in life
Of such allowance: were she mine at least,
So wonderful a wife, assuredly
She would companion me throughout my days
And never once bring sorrow!"
                              A great voice—
"My hosts here!"
                    Oh, the thrill that ran through us!
Never was aught so good and opportune
As that great interrupting voice! For see!
Here maundered this dispirited old age
Before the palace; whence a something crept
Which told us well enough without a word
What was a-doing inside,—every touch
O' the garland on those temples, tenderest
Disposure of each arm along its side,
Came putting out what warmth i' the world was left.
Then, as it happens at a sacrifice
When, drop by drop, some lustral bath is brimmed:
Into the thin and clear and cold, at once
They slaughter a whole wine-skin; Bacchos' blood
Sets the white water all aflame: even so,
Sudden into the midst of sorrow, leapt
Along with the gay cheer of that great voice,
Hope, joy, salvation: Herakles was here!
Himself, o' the threshold, sent his voice on first
To herald all that human and divine
I' the weary happy face of him,—half God,
Half man, which made the god-part God the more.

"Hosts mine," he broke upon the sorrow with,
"Inhabitants of this Pheraian soil,
Chance I upon Admetos inside here?"

The irresistible sound wholesome heart
O' the hero,—more than all the mightiness
At labor in the limbs that, for man's sake,
Labored and meant to labor their life-long,—
This drove back, dried up sorrow at its source.
How could it brave the happy weary laugh
Of who had bantered sorrow, "Sorrow here?
What have you done to keep your friend from harm?
Could no one give the life I see he keeps?
Or, say there 's sorrow here past friendly help,
Why waste a word or let a tear escape

While other sorrows wait you in the world,
And want the life of you, though helpless here?"
Clearly there was no telling such an one
How, when their monarch tried who loved him more
Than he loved them, and found they loved, as he,
Each man, himself, and held, no otherwise,
That, of all evils in the world, the worst
Was—being forced to die, whate'er death gain:
How all this selfishness in him and them
Caused certain sorrow which they sang about,—
I think that Herakles, who held his life
Out on his hand, for any man to take—
I think his laugh had marred their threnody.

"He is in the house," they answered. After all,
They might have told the story, talked their best
About the inevitable sorrow here,
Nor changed nor cheeked the kindly nature,—no!
So long as men were merely weak, not bad,
He loved men: were they Gods he used to help?
"Yea, Pheres' son is in-doors, Herakles.
But say, what sends thee to Thessalian soil,
Brought by what business to this Pherai town?"

"A certain labor that I have to do
Eurustheus the Tirunthian," laughed the God.

"And whither wendest—on what wandering
Bound now?" (They had an instinct, guessed what meant
Wanderings, labors, in the God's light mouth.)

"After the Thrakian Diomedes' car
With the four horses."

                    "Ah, but canst thou that?
Art inexperienced in thy host to be?"

"All-inexperienced: I have never gone
As yet to the land o' the Bistones."

                        "Then, look
By no means to be master of the steeds
Without a battle!"
                    "Battle there may be:
I must refuse no labor, all the same."

"Certainly, either having slain a foe
Wilt thou return to us, or, slain thyself,

Stay there!"
          "And, even if the game be so,
The risk in it were not the first I run."

"But, say thou overpower the lord o' the place,
What more advantage dost expect thereby?"

"I shall drive off his horses to the king."

"No easy handling them to bit the jaw!"

"Easy enough; except, at least, they breathe
Fire from their nostrils!"
                    "But they mince up men
With those quick jaws!"
"You talk of provender
For mountain-beasts, and not mere horses' food!"

"Thou mayst behold their mangers caked with gore!"

"And of what sire does he who bred them boast
Himself the son?"
              "Of Ares, king o' the targe—
Thrakian, of gold throughout."
                        Another laugh.
"Why, just the labor, just the lot for me
Dost thou describe in what I recognize!
Since hard and harder, high and higher yet,
Truly this lot of mine is like to go
If I must needs join battle with the brood
Of Ares: ay, I fought Lukaon first,
And again, Kuknos: now engage in strife
This third time, with such horses and such lord.
But there is nobody shall ever see
Alkmené's son shrink foemen's hand before!"

—"Or ever hear him say" (the Chorus thought)
"That death is terrible; and help us so
To chime in—'terrible beyond a doubt,
And, if to thee, why, to ourselves much more:
Know what has happened, then, and sympathize'!"
Therefore they gladly stopped the dialogue,
Shifted the burden to new shoulder straight,
As, "Look where comes the lord o' the land, himself,
Admetos, from the palace!" they outbroke
In some surprise, as well as much relief.
What had induced the king to waive his right
And luxury of woe in loneliness?

Out he came quietly; the hair was clipt,
And the garb sable; else no outward sign
Of sorrow as he came and faced his friend.
Was truth fast terrifying tears away?
"Hail, child of Zeus, and sprung from Perseus too!"
The salutation ran without a fault.

"And thou, Admetos, King of Thessaly!"

"Would, as thou wishest me, the grace might fall!
But my good-wisher, that thou art, I know."

"What 's here? these shorn locks, this sad show of thee?"

"I must inter a certain corpse to-day."

"Now, from thy children God avert mischance!"

"They live, my children; all are in the house!"

"Thy father—if 't is he departs indeed,
His age was ripe at least."

               "My father lives,
And she who bore me lives too, Herakles."

"It cannot be thy wife Alkestis gone?"

"Twofold the tale is, I can tell of her."

"Dead dost thou speak of her, or living yet?"

"She is—and is not: hence the pain to me!"

"I learn no whit the more, so dark thy speech!"

"Know'st thou not on what fate she needs must fall?"

"I know she is resigned to die for thee."

"How lives she still, then, if submitting so?"

"Eh, weep her not beforehand! wait till then!"

"Who is to die is dead; doing is done."

"To be and not to be are thought diverse."

"Thou judgest this—I, that way, Herakles!"

"Well, but declare what causes thy complaint!
Who is the man has died from out thy friends?"

"No man: I had a woman in my mind."

"Alien, or some one born akin to thee?"

"Alien: but still related to my house."

"How did it happen then that here she died?"

"Her father dying left his orphan here."

"Alas, Admetos—would we found thee gay,
Not grieving!"

       "What as if about to do
Subjoinest thou that comment?"
              "I shall seek
Another hearth, proceed to other hosts."

"Never, O king, shall that be! No such ill
Betide me!"
       "Nay, to mourners should there come
A guest, he proves importunate!"
"The dead—
Dead are they: but go thou within my house!"

"'T is base carousing beside friends who mourn."

"The guest-rooms, whither we shall lead thee, lie
Apart from ours."
       "Nay, let me go my way!
Ten-thousandfold the favor I shall thank!"

"It may not be thou goest to the hearth
Of any man but me!" so made an end
Admetos, softly and decisively,
Of the altercation. Herakles forbore:
And the king bade a servant lead the way,
Open the guest-rooms ranged remote from view
O' the main hall, tell the functionaries, next,
They had to furnish forth a plenteous feast:
And then shut close the doors o' the hall, midway,
"Because it is not proper friends who feast

Should hear a groaning or be grieved," quoth he.

Whereat the hero, who was truth itself,
Let out the smile again, repressed awhile
Like fountain-brilliance one forbids to play.
He did too many grandnesses, to note
Much in the meaner things about his path:
And stepping there, with face towards the sun,
Stopped seldom, to pluck weeds or ask their names.
Therefore he took Admetos at the word:
This trouble must not hinder any more
A true heart from good will and pleasant ways.
And so, the great arm, which had slain the snake,
Strained his friend's head a moment in embrace
On that broad breast beneath the lion's hide,
Till the king's cheek winced at the thick rough gold;
And then strode off, with who had care of him,
To the remote guest-chamber: glad to give
Poor flesh and blood their respite and relief
In the interval 'twixt fight and fight again—
All for the world's sake. Our eyes followed him,
Be sure, till those mid-doors shut us outside.
The king, too, watched great Herakles go off
All faith, love, and obedience to a friend.

And when they questioned him, the simple ones,
"What dost thou? Such calamity to face,
Lies full before thee—and thou art so bold
As play the host, Admetos? Hast thy wits?"
He replied calmly to each chiding tongue:
"But if from house and home I forced away
A coming guest, wouldst thou have praised me more?
No, truly! since calamity were mine,
Nowise diminished: while I showed myself
Unhappy and inhospitable too:
So adding to my ills this other ill,
That mine were styled a stranger-hating house.
Myself have ever found this man the best
Of entertainers when I went his way
To parched and thirsty Argos."
                    "If so be—
Why didst thou hide what destiny was here,
When one came that was kindly, as thou say'st?"

"He never would have willed to cross my door
Had he known aught of my calamities.
And probably to some of you I seem
Unwise enough in doing what I do;

Such will scarce praise me: but these halls of mine
Know not to drive off and dishonor guests."

And so, the duty done, he turned once more
To go and busy him about his dead.
As for the sympathizers left to muse,
There was a change, a new light thrown on things,
Contagion from the magnanimity
O' the man whose life lay on his hand so light,
As up he stepped, pursuing duty still
"Higher and harder," as he laughed and said.
Somehow they found no folly now in the act
They blamed erewhile: Admetos' private grief
Shrank to a somewhat pettier obstacle
I' the way o' the world: they saw good days had been,
And good days, peradventure, still might be,
Now that they overlooked the present cloud
Heavy upon the palace opposite.
And soon the thought took words and music thus:—

"Harbor of many a stranger, free to friend,
Ever and always, O thou house o' the man
We mourn for! Thee, Apollon's very self,
The lyric Puthian, deigned inhabit once,
Become a shepherd here in thy domains,
And pipe, adown the winding hillside paths,
Pastoral marriage-poems to thy flocks
At feed: while with them fed in fellowship,
Through joy i' the music, spot-skin lynxes; ay,
And lions too, the bloody company,
Came, leaving Othrus' dell; and round thy lyre,
Phoibos, there danced the speckle-coated fawn,
Pacing on lightsome fetlock past the pines
Tress-topped, the creature's natural boundary
Into the open everywhere; such heart
Had she within her, beating joyous beats,
At the sweet reassurance of thy song!
Therefore the lot o' the master is, to live
In a home multitudinous with herds,
Along by the fair-flowing Boibian lake,
Limited, that ploughed land and pasture-plain,
Only where stand the sun's steeds, stabled west
I' the cloud, by that mid-air which makes the clime
Of those Molossoi: and he rules as well
O'er the Aigaian, up to Pelion's shore,—
Sea-stretch without a port! Such lord have we:
And here he opens house now, as of old,
Takes to the heart of it a guest again:

Though moist the eyelid of the master, still
Mourning his dear wife's body, dead but now!"

And they admired: nobility of soul
Was self-impelled to reverence, they saw:
The best men ever prove the wisest too:
Something instinctive guides them still aright.
And on each soul this boldness settled now,
That one who reverenced the Gods so much
Would prosper yet: (or—I could wish it ran—
Who venerates the Gods i' the main will still
Practise things honest though obscure to judge).

They ended, for Admetos entered now;
Having disposed all duteously indoors,
He came into the outside world again,
Quiet as ever: but a quietude
Bent on pursuing its descent to truth,
As who must grope until he gain the ground
O' the dungeon doomed to be his dwelling now.
Already high o'er head was piled the dusk,
When something pushed to stay his downward step,
Pluck back despair just reaching its repose.
He would have bidden the kind presence there
Observe that,—since the corpse was coming out,
Cared for in all things that befit the case,
Carried aloft, in decency and state,
To the last burial-place and burning pile,—
'T were proper friends addressed, as custom prompts,
Alkestis bound on her last journeying.

"Ay, for we see thy father," they subjoined,
"Advancing as the aged foot best may;
His servants, too: each bringing in his hand
Adornments for thy wife, all pomp that 's due
To the downward-dwelling people." And in truth,
By slow procession till they filled the stage,
Came Pheres, and his following, and their gifts.
You see, the worst of the interruption was,
It plucked back, with an over-hasty hand,
Admetos from descending to the truth,
(I told you)—put him on the brink again,
Full i' the noise and glare where late he stood:
With no fate fallen and irrevocable,
But all things subject still to chance and change:
And that chance—life, and that change—happiness.
And with the low strife came the little mind:
He was once more the man might gain so much,

Life too and wife too, would his friends but help!
All he felt now was that there faced him one
Supposed the likeliest, in emergency,
To help: and help, by mere self-sacrifice
So natural, it seemed as if the sire
Must needs lie open still to argument,
Withdraw the rash decision, not to die
But rather live, though death would save his son:—
Argument like the ignominious grasp
O' the drowner whom his fellow grasps as fierce,
Each marvelling that the other needs must hold
Head out of water, though friend choke thereby.

And first the father's salutation fell.
Burdened he came, in common with his child,
Who lost, none would gainsay, a good chaste spouse:
Yet such things must be borne, though hard to bear.
"So, take this tribute of adornment, deep
In the earth let it descend along with her!
Behooves we treat the body with respect
—Of one who died, at least, to save thy life,
Kept me from being childless, nor allowed
That I, bereft of thee, should peak and pine
In melancholy age! she, for the sex,
All of her sisters, put in evidence,
By daring such a feat, that female life
Might prove more excellent than men suppose.
O thou Alkestis!" out he burst in fine,
"Who, while thou savedst this my son, didst raise
Also myself from sinking,—hail to thee!
Well be it with thee even in the house
Of Hades! I maintain, if mortals must
Marry, this sort of marriage is the sole
Permitted those among them who are wise!"

So his oration ended. Like hates like:
Accordingly Admetos,—full i' the face
Of Pheres, his true father, outward shape
And inward fashion, body matching soul,—
Saw just himself when years should do their work
And reinforce the selfishness inside
Until it pushed the last disguise away:
As when the liquid metal cools i' the mould,
Stands forth a statue: bloodless, hard, cold bronze.
So, in old Pheres, young Admetos showed,
Pushed to completion: and a shudder ran,
And his repugnance soon had vent in speech:
Glad to escape outside, nor, pent within,

Find itself there fit food for exercise.

"Neither to this interment called by me
Comest thou, nor thy presence I account
Among the covetable proofs of love.
As for thy tribute of adornment,—no!
Ne'er shall she don it, ne'er in debt to thee
Be buried! What is thine, that keep thou still!
Then it behooved thee to commiserate
When I was perishing: but thou—who stood'st
Foot-free o' the snare, wast acquiescent then
That I, the young, should die, not thou, the old—
Wilt thou lament this corpse thyself hast slain?
Thou wast not, then, true father to this flesh;
Nor she, who makes profession of my birth
And styles herself my mother, neither she
Bore me: but, come of slave's blood, I was cast
Stealthily 'neath the bosom of thy wife!
Thou showedst, put to touch, the thing thou art,
Nor I esteem myself born child of thee!
Otherwise, thine is the preëminence
O'er all the world in cowardice of soul:
Who, being the old man thou art, arrived
Where life should end, didst neither will nor dare
Die for thy son, but left the task to her,
The alien woman, whom I well might think
Own, only mother both and father too!
And yet a fair strife had been thine to strive,
—Dying for thy own child; and brief for thee
In any case, the rest of time to live;
While I had lived, and she, our rest of time,
Nor I been left to groan in solitude.
Yet certainly all things which happy man
Ought to experience, thy experience grasped.
Thou wast a ruler through the bloom of youth,
And I was son to thee, recipient due
Of sceptre and demesne,—no need to fear
That dying thou shouldst leave an orphan house
For strangers to despoil. Nor yet wilt thou
Allege that as dishonoring, forsooth,
Thy length of days, I gave thee up to die,—
I, who have held thee in such reverence!
And in exchange for it, such gratitude
Thou, father,—thou award'st me, mother mine!
Go, lose no time, then, in begetting sons
Shall cherish thee in age, and, when thou diest,
Deck up and lay thee out as corpses claim!
For never I, at least, with this my hand

Will bury thee: it is myself am dead
So far as lies in thee. But if I light
Upon another savior, and still see
The sunbeam,—his, the child I call myself,
His, the old age that claims my cherishing.
How vainly do these aged pray for death,
Abuse the slow drag of senility!
But should death step up, nobody inclines
To die, nor age is now the weight it was!"

You see what all this poor pretentious talk
Tried at,—how weakness strove to hide itself
In bluster against weakness,—the loud word
To hide the little whisper, not so low
Already in that heart beneath those lips!
Ha, could it be, who hated cowardice
Stood confessed craven, and who lauded so
Self-immolating love, himself had pushed
The loved one to the altar in his place?
Friends interposed, would fain stop further play
O' the sharp-edged tongue: they felt love's champion here
Had left an undefended point or two,
The antagonist might profit by; bade "Pause!
Enough the present sorrow! Nor, O son,
Whet thus against thyself thy father's soul!"

Ay, but old Pheres was the stouter stuff!
Admetos, at the flintiest of the heart,
Had so much soft in him as held a fire:
The other was all iron, clashed from flint
Its fire, but shed no spark and showed no bruise.
Did Pheres crave instruction as to facts?
He came, content, the ignoble word, for him,
Should lurk still in the blackness of each breast,
As sleeps the water-serpent half surmised:
Not brought up to the surface at a bound,
By one touch of the idly-probing spear,
Reed-like against unconquerable scale.
He came pacific, rather, as strength should,
Bringing the decent praise, the due regret,
And each banality prescribed of old.
Did he commence "Why let her die for you?"
And rouse the coiled and quiet ugliness,
"What is so good to man as man's own life?"
No: but the other did: and, for his pains,
Out, full in face of him, the venom leapt.

"And whom dost thou make bold, son—Ludian slave,

Or Phrugian whether, money made thy ware,
To drive at with revilings? Know'st thou not
I, a Thessalian, from Thessalian sire
Spring and am born legitimately free?
Too arrogant art thou; and, youngster words
Casting against me, having had thy fling,
Thou goest not off as all were ended so!
I gave thee birth indeed and mastership
I' the mansion, brought thee up to boot: there ends
My owing, nor extends to die for thee!
Never did I receive it as a law
Hereditary, no, nor Greek at all,
That sires in place of sons were hound to die.
For, to thy sole and single self wast thou
Born, with whatever fortune, good or bad;
Such things as bear bestowment, those thou hast;
Already ruling widely, broad lands, too,
Doubt not but I shall leave thee in due time:
For why? My father left me them before.
Well then, where wrong I thee?—of what defraud?
Neither do thou die for this man, myself,
Nor let him die for thee!—is all I beg.
Thou joyest seeing daylight: dost suppose
Thy father Joys not too? Undoubtedly,
Long I account the time to pass below,
And brief my span of days; yet sweet the same:
Is it otherwise to thee who, impudent,
Didst fight off this same death, and livest now
Through having sneaked past fate apportioned thee,
And slain thy wife so? Cryest cowardice
On me, I wonder, thou—whom, poor poltroon,
A very woman worsted, daring death
Just for the sake of thee, her handsome spark?
Shrewdly hast thou contrived how not to die
Forevermore now: 't is but still persuade
The wife, for the time being, to take thy place!
What, and thy friends who would not do the like,
These dost thou carp at, craven thus thyself?
Crouch and be silent, craven! Comprehend
That, if thou lovest so that life of thine,
Why, everybody loves his own life too:
So, good words, henceforth! If thou speak us ill,
Many and true an ill thing shalt thou hear!"

There you saw leap the hydra at full length!
Only, the old kept glorying the more,
The more the portent thus uncoiled itself,
Whereas the young man shuddered head to foot,

And shrank from kinship with the creature. Why
Such horror, unless what he hated most,
Vaunting itself outside, might fairly claim
Acquaintance with the counterpart at home?
I would the Chorus here had plucked up heart,
Spoken out boldly and explained the man,
If not to men, to Gods. That way, I think,
Sophokles would have led their dance and song.
Here, they said simply, "Too much evil spoke
On both sides!" As the young before, so now
They bade the old man leave abusing thus.

"Let him speak,—I have spoken!" said the youth:
And so died out the wrangle by degrees,
In wretched bickering. "If thou wince at fact,
Behooved thee not prove faulty to myself!"

"Had I died for thee I had faulted more!"

"All 's one, then, for youth's bloom and age to die?"

"Our duty is to live one life, not two!"

"Go then, and outlive Zeus, for aught I care!"

"What, curse thy parents with no sort of cause?"

"Curse, truly! All thou lovest is long life!"

"And dost not thou, too, all for love of life,
Carry out now, in place of thine, this corpse?"

"Monument, rather, of thy cowardice,
Thou worst one!"

       "Not for me she died, I hope!
That, thou wilt hardly say!"
             "No; simply this:
Would, some day, thou mayst come to need myself!"

"Meanwhile, woo many wives—the more will die!"

"And so shame thee who never dared the like!"

"Dear is this light o' the sun-god—dear, I say!"

"Proper conclusion for a beast to draw!"

"One thing is certain: there 's no laughing now,
As out thou bearest the poor dead old man!"

"Die when thou wilt, thou wilt die infamous!"

"And once dead, whether famed or infamous,
I shall not care!"
        "Alas and yet again!
How full is age of impudency!"
          "True!
Thou couldst not call thy young wife impudent:
She was found foolish merely."

        "Get thee gone!
And let me bury this my dead!"
          "I go.
Thou buriest her whom thou didst murder first;
Whereof there 's some account to render yet
Those kinsfolk by the marriage-side! I think,
Brother Akastos may be classed with me,
Among the beasts, not men, if he omit
Avenging upon thee his sister's blood!"

"Go to perdition, with thy housemate too!
Grow old all childlessly, with child alive,
Just as ye merit! for to me, at least,
Beneath the same roof ne'er do ye return.
And did I need by heralds' help renounce
The ancestral hearth, I had renounced the same!
But we—since this woe, lying at our feet
I' the path, is to be borne—let us proceed
And lay the body on the pyre."
        I think,
What, through this wretched wrangle, kept the man
From seeing clear—beside the cause I gave—
Was, that the woe, himself described as full
I' the path before him, there did really lie—
Not roll into the abyss of dead and gone.
How, with Alkestis present, calmly crowned,
Was she so irrecoverable yet—
The bird, escaped, that 's just on bough above,
The flower, let flutter half-way down the brink?
Not so detached seemed lifelessness from life
But—one dear stretch beyond all straining yet—
And he might have her at his heart once more,
When, in the critical minute, up there comes
The father and the fact, to trifle time!

"To the pyre!" an instinct prompted: pallid face,
And passive arm and pointed foot, when these
No longer shall absorb the sight, O friends,
Admetos will begin to see indeed
Who the true foe was, where the blows should fall!

So, the old selfish Pheres went his way,
Case-hardened as he came; and left the youth,
(Only half selfish now, since sensitive)
To go on learning by a light the more,
As friends moved off, renewing dirge the while:

"Unhappy in thy daring! Noble dame,
Best of the good, farewell! With favoring face
May Hermes the infernal, Hades too,
Receive thee! And if there,—ay, there,—some touch
Of further dignity await the good,
Sharing with them, mayst thou sit throned by her
The Bride of Hades, in companionship!"

Wherewith, the sad procession wound away,
Made slowly for the suburb sepulchre.
And lo,—while still one's heart, in time and tune,
Paced after that symmetric step of Death
Mute-marching, to the mind's eye, at the head
O' the mourners—one hand pointing out their path
With the long pale terrific sword we saw.
The other leading, with grim tender grace,
Alkestis quieted and consecrate,—
Lo, life again knocked laughing at the door!
The world goes on, goes ever, in and through,
And out again o' the cloud. We faced about.
Fronted the palace where the mid-hall gate
Opened—not half, nor half of half, perhaps—
Yet wide enough to let out light and life,
And warmth, and bounty, and hope, and joy, at once.
Festivity burst wide, fruit rare and ripe
Crushed in the mouth of Bacchos, pulpy-prime,
All juice and flavor, save one single seed
Duly ejected from the God's nice lip,
Which lay o' the red edge, blackly visible—
To wit, a certain ancient servitor:
On whom the festal jaws o' the palace shut,
So, there he stood, a much-bewildered man.
Stupid? Nay, but sagacious in a sort:
Learned, life-long, i' the first outside of things,
Though bat for blindness to what lies beneath
And needs a nail-scratch ere 't is laid you bare.

This functionary was the trusted one
We saw deputed by Admetos late
To lead in Herakles and help him, soul
And body, to such snatched repose, snapped-up
Sustainment, as might do away the dust
O' the last encounter, knit each nerve anew
For that next onset sure to come at cry
O' the creature next assailed,—nay, should it prove
Only the creature that came forward now
To play the critic upon Herakles!

"Many the guests,"—so he soliloquized
In musings burdensome to breast before,
When it seemed not too prudent tongue should wag,—
"Many, and from all quarters of this world,
The guests I now have known frequent our house,
For whom I spread the banquet; but than this,
Never a worse one did I yet receive
At the hearth here! One who seeing, first of all,
The master's sorrow, entered gate the same,
And had the hardihood to house himself.
Did things stop there! But, modest by no means,
He took what entertainment lay to hand,
Knowing of our misfortune,—did we fail
In aught of the fit service, urged us serve
Just as a guest expects! And in his hands
Taking the ivied goblet, drinks and drinks
The unmixed product of black mother-earth,
Until the blaze o' the wine went round about
And warmed him: then he crowns with myrtle sprigs
His head, and howls discordance—twofold lay
Was thereupon for us to listen to—
This fellow singing, namely, nor restrained
A jot by sympathy with sorrows here—
While we o' the household mourned our mistress—mourned,
That is to say, in silence—never showed
The eyes, which we kept wetting, to the guest—
For there Admetos was imperative.
And so, here am I helping make at home
A guest, some fellow ripe for wickedness,
Robber or pirate, while she goes her way
Out of our house: and neither was it mine
To follow in procession, nor stretch forth
Hand, wave my lady dear a last farewell,
Lamenting who to me and all of us
Domestics was a mother: myriad harms
She used to ward away from every one,
And mollify her husband's ireful mood.

I ask then, do I justly hate or no
This guest, this interloper on our grief?"

"Hate him and justly!" Here 's the proper judge
Of what is due to the house from Herakles!
This man of much experience saw the first
O' the feeble duckings-down at destiny,
When King Admetos went his rounds, poor soul,
A-begging somebody to be so brave
As die for one afraid to die himself—
"Thou, friend? Thou, love? Father or mother, then!
None of you? What, Alkestis must Death catch?
O best of wives, one woman in the world!
But nowise droop: our prayers may still assist:
Let us try sacrifice; if those avail
Nothing and Gods avert their countenance,
Why, deep and durable our grief will be!"
Whereat the house, this worthy at its head,
Re-echoed "deep and durable our grief!"
This sage, who justly hated Herakles,
Did he suggest once "Rather I than she!"
Admonish the Turannos—"Be a man!
Bear thine own burden, never think to thrust
Thy fate upon another and thy wife!
It were a dubious gain could death be doomed
That other, and no passionatest plea
Of thine, to die instead, have force with fate;
Seeing thou lov'st Alkestis: what were life
Unlighted by the loved one? But to live—
Not merely live unsolaced by some thought,
Some word so poor—yet solace all the same—
As 'Thou i' the sepulchre, Alkestis, say!
Would I, or would not I, to save thy life,
Die, and die on, and die forevermore?'
No! but to read red-written up and down
The world 'This is the sunshine, this the shade,
This is some pleasure of earth, sky or sea,
Due to that other, dead that thou mayst live!'
Such were a covetable gain to thee?
Go die, fool, and be happy while 't is time!"
One word of counsel in this kind, methinks,
Had fallen to better purpose than Ai, ai,
Pheu, pheu, e, papai, and a pother of praise
O' the best, best, best one! Nothing was to hate
In King Admetos, Pheres, and the rest
O' the household down to his heroic self!
This was the one thing hateful: Herakles
Had flung into the presence, frank and free,

Out from the labor into the repose,
Ere out again and over head and ears
I' the heart of labor, all for love of men:
Making the most o' the minute, that the soul
And body, strained to height a minute since,
Might lie relaxed in joy, this breathing-space,
For man's sake more than ever; till the bow,
Restrung o' the sudden, at first cry for help,
Should send some unimaginable shaft
True to the aim and shatteringly through
The plate-mail of a monster, save man so.
He slew the pest o' the marish yesterday:
To-morrow he would bit the flame-breathed stud
That fed on man's-flesh: and this day between—
Because he held it natural to die,
And fruitless to lament a thing past cure,
So, took his fill of food, wine, song and flowers,
Till the new labor claimed him soon enough,—
"Hate him and justly!"
            True, Charopé mine!
The man surmised not Herakles lay hid
I' the guest; or, knowing it, was ignorant
That still his lady lived—for Herakles;
Or else judged lightness needs must indicate
This or the other caitiff quality:
And therefore—had been right if not so wrong!
For who expects the sort of him will scratch
A nail's depth, scrape the surface just to see
What peradventure underlies the same?

So, he stood petting up his puny hate,
Parent-wise, proud of the ill-favored babe.
Not long! A great hand, careful lest it crush,
Startled him on the shoulder: up he stared,
And over him, who stood but Herakles!
There smiled the mighty presence, all one smile
And no touch more of the world-weary God,
Through the brief respite. Just a garland's grace
About the brow, a song to satisfy
Head, heart and breast, and trumpet-lips at once,
A solemn draught of true religious wine,
And—how should I know?—half a mountain-goat
Tom up and swallowed down,—the feast was fierce
But brief: all cares and pains took wing and flew,
Leaving the hero ready to begin
And help mankind, whatever woe came next,
Even though what came next should be naught more
Than the mean querulous mouth o' the man, remarked

Pursing its grievance up till patience failed
And the sage needs must rush out, as we saw,
To sulk outside and pet his hate in peace.
By no means would the Helper have it so:
He who was just about to handle brutes
In Thrace, and bit the jaws which breathed the flame,—
Well, if a good laugh and a jovial word
Could bridle age which blew bad humors forth,
That were a kind of help, too!
                           "Thou, there!" hailed
This grand benevolence the ungracious one—
"Why look'st so solemn and so thought-absorbed?
To guests a servant should not sour-faced be,
But do the honors with a mind urbane.
While thou, contrariwise, beholding here
Arrive thy master's comrade, hast for him
A churlish visage, all one beetle-brow—
Having regard to grief that's out-of-door!
Come hither, and so get to grow more wise!
Things mortal—know'st the nature that they have?
No, I imagine! whence could knowledge spring?
Give ear to me, then! For all flesh to die,
Is Nature's due; nor is there any one
Of mortals with assurance he shall last
The coming morrow: for, what 's born of chance
Invisibly proceeds the way it will,
Not to be learned, no fortune-teller's prize.
This, therefore, having heard and known through me,
Gladden thyself! Drink! Count the day-by-day
Existence thine, and all the other—chance!
Ay, and pay homage also to by far
The sweetest of divinities for man,
Kupris! Benignant Goddess will she prove!
But as for aught else, leave and let things be!
And trust my counsel, if I seem to speak
To purpose—as I do, apparently.
Wilt not thou, then,—discarding overmuch
Mournfulness, do away with this shut door,
Come drink along with me, be-garlanded
This fashion? Do so, and—I well know what—
From this stern mood, this shrunk-up state of mind,
The pit-pat fall o' the flagon-juice down throat,
Soon will dislodge thee from bad harborage!
Men being mortal should think mortal-like:
Since to your solemn, brow-contracting sort,
All of them,—so I lay down law at least,—
Life is not truly life but misery."

Whereto the man with softened surliness:
"We know as much: but deal with matters, now,
Hardly befitting mirth and revelry."

"No intimate, this woman that is dead:
Mourn not too much! For, those o' the house itself,
Thy masters live, remember!"

                    "Live indeed?
Ah, thou know'st naught o' the woe within these walls!"

"I do—unless thy master spoke me false
Somehow!"
          "Ay, ay, too much he loves a guest,
Too much, that master mine!" so muttered he.

"Was it improper he should treat me well,
Because an alien corpse was in the way?"

"No alien, but most intimate indeed!"

"Can it be, some woe was, he told me not?"

"Farewell and go thy way! Thy cares for thee—
To us, our master's sorrow is a care."

"This word begins no tale of alien woe!"

"Had it been other woe than intimate,
I could have seen thee feast, nor felt amiss."

"What! have I suffered strangely from my host?"

"Thou cam'st not at a fit reception-time:
With sorrow here beforehand: and thou seest
Shorn hair, black robes."
                    "But who is it that 's dead?
Some child gone? or the aged sire perhaps?"

"Admetos' wife, then! she has perished, guest!"

"How sayest? And did ye house me, all the same?"

"Ay: for he had thee in that reverence
He dared not turn thee from his door away!"

"O hapless, and bereft of what a mate!"

"All of us now are dead, not she alone!"

"But I divined it! seeing, as I did,
His eye that ran with tears, his close-clipt hair,
His countenance! Though he persuaded me,
Saying it was a stranger's funeral
He went with to the grave: against my wish,
He forced on me that I should enter doors,
Drink in the hall o' the hospitable man
Circumstanced so! And do I revel yet
With wreath on head? But—thou to hold thy peace,
Nor me what a woe oppressed my friend!
Where is he gone to bury her? Where am I
To go and find her?"
                    "By the road that leads
Straight to Larissa, thou wilt see the tomb,
Out of the suburb, a carved sepulchre."

So said he, and therewith dismissed himself
Inside to his lamenting: somewhat soothed,
However, that he had adroitly spoilt
The mirth of the great creature: oh, he marked
The movement of the mouth, how lip pressed lip,
And either eye forgot to shine, as, fast,
He plucked the chaplet from his forehead, dashed
The myrtle-sprays down, trod them underfoot!
And all the joy and wonder of the wine
Withered away, like fire from off a brand
The wind blows over—beacon though it be,
Whose merry ardor only meant to make
Somebody all the better for its blaze,
And save lost people in the dark: quenched now!

Not long quenched! As the flame, just hurried off
The brand's edge, suddenly renews its bite,
Tasting some richness caked i' the core o' the tree,—
Pine, with a blood that 's oil,—and triumphs up
Pillar-wise to the sky and saves the world:
So, in a spasm and splendor of resolve,
All at once did the God surmount the man.

"O much-enduring heart and hand of mine!
Now show what sort of son she bore to Zeus,
That daughter of Elektruon, Tiruns' child,
Alkmené! for that son must needs save now
The just-dead lady: ay, establish here
I' the house again Alkestis, bring about
Comfort and succor to Admetos so!

I will go lie in wait for Death, black-stoled
King of the corpses! I shall find him, sure,
Drinking, beside the tomb, o' the sacrifice:
And if I lie in ambuscade, and leap
Out of my lair, and seize—encircle him
Till one hand join the other round about—
There lives not who shall pull him out from me,
Rib-mauled, before he let the woman go!
But even say I miss the booty,—say,
Death comes not to the boltered blood,—why then,
Down go I, to the unsunned dwelling-place
Of Koré and the king there,—make demand,
Confident I shall bring Alkestis back,
So as to put her in the hands of him
My host, that housed me, never drove me off:
Though stricken with sore sorrow, hid the stroke,
Being a noble heart and honoring me!
Who of Thessalians, more than this man, loves
The stranger? Who, that now inhabits Greece?
Wherefore he shall not say the man was vile
Whom he befriended,—native noble heart!"

So, one look upward, as if Zeus might laugh
Approval of his human progeny,—
One summons of the whole magnific frame,
Each sinew to its service,—up he caught,
And over shoulder cast, the lion-shag,
Let the club go,—for had he not those hands?
And so went striding off, on that straight way
Leads to Larissa and the suburb tomb.
Gladness be with thee, Helper of our world!
I think this is the authentic sign and seal
Of Godship, that it ever waxes glad,
And more glad, until gladness blossoms, bursts
Into a rage to suffer for mankind,
And recommence at sorrow: drops like seed
After the blossom, ultimate of all.
Say, does the seed scorn earth and seek the sun?
Surely it has no other end and aim
Than to drop, once more die into the ground,
Taste cold and darkness and oblivion there:
And thence rise, tree-like grow through pain to joy,
More joy and most joy,—do man good again.

So, to the struggle off strode Herakles.
When silence closed behind the lion-garb,
Back came our dull fact settling in its place,
Though heartiness and passion half-dispersed

The inevitable fate. And presently
In came the mourners from the funeral,
One after one, until we hoped the last
Would be Alkestis and so end our dream.
Could they have really left Alkestis lone
I' the wayside sepulchre! Home, all save she!
And when Admetos felt that it was so,
By the stand-still: when he lifted head and face
From the two hiding hands and peplos' fold,
And looked forth, knew the palace, knew the hills,
Knew the plains, knew the friendly frequence there,
And no Alkestis any more again,
Why, the whole woe billow-like broke on him.

"O hateful entry, hateful countenance
O' the widowed halls!"—he moaned. "What was to be?
Go there? Stay here? Speak, not speak? All was now
Mad and impossible alike; one way
And only one was sane and safe—to die:
Now he was made aware how dear is death,
How lovable the dead are, how the heart
Yearns in us to go hide where they repose,
When we find sunbeams do no good to see,
Nor earth rests rightly where our footsteps fall.
His wife had been to him the very pledge,
Sun should be sun, earth—earth; the pledge was robbed,
Pact broken, and the world was left no world."
He stared at the impossible, mad life:
Stood, while they urged "Advance—advance! Go deep
Into the utter dark, thy palace-core!"
They tried what they called comfort, "touched the quick
Of the ulceration in his soul," he said,
With memories,—"once thy joy was thus and thus!"
True comfort were to let him fling himself
Into the hollow grave o' the tomb, and so
Let him lie dead along with all he loved.

One bade him note that his own family
Boasted a certain father whose sole son,
Worthy bewailment, died: and yet the sire
Bore stoutly up against the blow and lived;
For all that he was childless now, and prone
Already to gray hairs, far on in life.
Could such a good example miss effect?
Why fix foot, stand so, staring at the house,
Why not go in, as that wise kinsman would?

"Oh that arrangement of the house I know!

How can I enter, how inhabit thee
Now that one cast of fortune changes all?
Oh me, for much divides the then from now!
Then—with those pine-tree torches, Pelian pomp
And marriage-hymns, I entered, holding high
The hand of my dear wife; while many-voiced
The revelry that followed me and her
That 's dead now,—friends felicitating both,
As who were lofty-lineaged, each of us
Born of the best, two wedded and made one;
Now—wail is wedding-chant's antagonist,
And, for white peplos, stoles in sable state
Herald my way to the deserted couch!"

The one word more they ventured was, "This grief
Befell thee witless of what sorrow means,
Close after prosperous fortune: but, reflect!
Thou hast saved soul and body. Dead, thy wife—
Living, the love she left. What 's novel here?
Many the man, from whom Death long ago
Loosed the life-partner!"
                    Then Admetos spoke:
Turned on the comfort, with no tears, this time.
He was beginning to be like his wife.
I told you of that pressure to the point,
Word slow pursuing word in monotone,
Alkestis spoke with; so Admetos, now,
Solemnly bore the burden of the truth.
And as the voice of him grew, gathered strength,
And groaned on, and persisted to the end,
We felt how deep had been descent in grief,
And with what change he came up now to light,
And left behind such littleness as tears.

"Friends, I account the fortune of my wife
Happier than mine, though it seem otherwise:
For, her indeed no grief will ever touch,
And she from many a labor pauses now,
Renowned one! Whereas I, who ought not live,
But do live, by evading destiny,
Sad life am I to lead, I learn at last!
For how shall I bear going in-doors here?
Accosting whom? By whom saluted back,
Shall I have joyous entry? Whither turn?
Inside, the solitude will drive me forth,
When I behold the empty bed—my wife's—
The seat she used to sit upon, the floor
Unsprinkled as when dwellers loved the cool,

The children that will clasp my knees about,
Cry for their mother back: these servants too
Moaning for what a guardian they have lost!
Inside my house such circumstance awaits,
Outside,—Thessalian people's marriage-feasts
And gatherings for talk will harass me,
With overflow of women everywhere;
It is impossible I look on them—
Familiars of my wife and just her age!
And then, whoever is a foe of mine,
And lights on me—why, this will be his word—
'See there! alive ignobly, there he skulks
That played the dastard when it came to die,
And, giving her he wedded, in exchange,
Kept himself out of Hades safe and sound,
The coward! Do you call that creature—man?
He hates his parents for declining death,
Just as if he himself would gladly die!'
This sort of reputation shall I have,
Beside the other ills enough in store.
Ill-famed, ill-faring,—what advantage, friends,
Do you perceive I gain by life for death?"

That was the truth. Vexed waters sank to smooth:
'T was only when the last of bubbles broke,
The latest circlet widened all away
And left a placid level, that up swam
To the surface the drowned truth, in dreadful change.
So, through the quiet and submission,—ay,
Spite of some strong words—(for you miss the tone)
The grief was getting to be infinite—
Grief, friends fell back before. Their office shrank
To that old solace of humanity!—
"Being born mortal, bear grief! Why born else?"
And they could only meditate anew.

"They, too, upborne by airy help of song.
And haply science, which can find the stars,
Had searched the heights: had sounded depths as well
By catching much at books where logic lurked,
Yet nowhere found they aught could overcome
Necessity; not any medicine served,
Which Thrakian tablets treasure, Orphic voice
Wrote itself down upon: nor remedy
Which Phoibos gave to the Asklepiadai;
Cutting the roots of many a virtuous herb
To solace overburdened mortals. None!
Of this sole goddess, never may we go

To altar nor to image: sacrifice
She hears not. All to pray for is—'Approach!
But, oh, no harder on me, awful one,
Than heretofore! Let life endure thee still!
For, whatsoe'er Zeus' nod decree, that same
In concert with thee hath accomplishment.
Iron, the very stuff o' the Chaluboi,
Thou, by sheer strength, dost conquer and subdue;
Nor, of that harsh abrupt resolve of thine,
Any relenting is there!"
                    "O my king!
Thee also, in the shackles of those hands,
Not to be shunned, the Goddess grasped! Yet, bear!
Since never wilt thou lead from underground
The dead ones, wail thy worst! If mortals die,—
The very children of immortals, too,
Dropped 'mid our darkness, these decay as sure!
Dear indeed was she while among us: dear,
Now she is dead, must she forever be:
Thy portion was to clasp, within thy couch,
The noblest of all women as a wife.
Nor be the tomb of her supposed some heap
That hides mortality: but like the Gods
Honored, a veneration to a world
Of wanderers! Oft the wanderer, struck thereby,
Who else had sailed past in his merchant-ship,
Ay, he shall leave ship, land, long wind his way
Up to the mountain-summit, till there break
Speech forth, 'So, this was she, then, died of old
To save her husband! now, a deity
She bends above us. Hail, benignant one!
Give good!' Such voices so will supplicate.
But—can it be? Alkmené's offspring comes,
Admetos!—to thy house advances here!"

I doubt not, they supposed him decently
Dead somewhere in that winter world of Thrace—
Vanquished by one o' the Bistones, or else
Victim to some mad steed's voracity—
For did not friends prognosticate as much?
It were a new example to the point,
That "children of immortals, dropped by stealth
Into our darkness, die as sure as we!"
A case to quote and comfort people with:
But, as for lamentation, ai and pheu,
Right-minded subjects kept them for their lord.

Ay, he it was advancing! In he strode,

And took his stand before Admetos,—turned
Now by despair to such a quietude,
He neither raised his face nor spoke, this time,
The while his friend surveyed him steadily.
That friend looked rough with fighting: had he strained
Worst brute to breast was ever strangled yet?
Somehow, a victory—for there stood the strength,
Happy, as always; something grave, perhaps
The great vein-cordage on the fret-worked front,
Black-swollen, beaded yet with battle-dew
The yellow hair o' the hero!—his big frame
A-quiver with each muscle sinking back
Into the sleepy smooth it leaped from late.
Under the great guard of one arm, there leant
A shrouded something, live and woman-like,
Propped by the heartbeats 'neath the lion-coat.
When he had finished his survey, it seemed,
The heavings of the heart began subside,
The helpful breath returned, and last the smile
Shone out, all Herakles was back again,
As the words followed the saluting hand.

"To friendly man, behooves we freely speak,
Admetos!—nor keep buried, deep in breast,
Blame we leave silent. I assuredly
Judged myself proper, if I should approach
By accident calamities of thine,
To be demonstrably thy friend: but thou
Told'st me not of the corpse then claiming care,
That was thy wife's, but didst instal me guest
I' the house here, as though busied with a grief
Indeed, but then, mere grief beyond thy gate:
And so, I crowned my head, and to the Gods
Poured my libations in thy dwelling-place,
With such misfortune round me. And I blame—
Certainly blame thee, having suffered thus!
But still I would not pain thee, pained enough:
So let it pass! Wherefore I seek thee now,
Having turned back again though onward bound,
That I will tell thee. Take and keep for me
This woman, till I come thy way again,
Driving before me, having killed the king
O' the Bistones, that drove of Thrakian steeds;
In such case, give the woman back to me!
But should I fare,—as fare I fain would not,
Seeing I hope to prosper and return,—
Then, I bequeath her as thy household slave.
She came into my hands with good hard toil!

For, what find I, when started on my course,
But certain people, a whole country-side,
Holding a wrestling-bout? as good to me
As a new labor: whence I took, and here
Come keeping with me, this, the victor's prize.
For, such as conquered in the easy work,
Gained horses which they drove away: and such
As conquered in the harder,—those who boxed
And wrestled,—cattle; and, to crown the prize,
A woman followed. Chancing as I did,
Base were it to forego this fame and gain!
Well, as I said, I trust her to thy care:
No woman I have kidnapped, understand!
But good hard toil has done it: here I come!
Some day, who knows? even thou wilt praise the feat!"

Admetos raised his face and eyed the pair:
Then, hollowly and with submission, spoke,
And spoke again, and spoke time after time,
When he perceived the silence of his friend
Would not be broken by consenting word.
As a tired slave goes adding stone to stone
Until he stop some current that molests,
So poor Admetos piled up argument
Vainly against the purpose all too plain
In that great brow acquainted with command.

"Nowise dishonoring, nor amid my foes
Ranking thee, did I hide my wife's ill fate;
But it were grief superimposed on grief,
Shouldst thou have hastened to another home.
My own woe was enough for me to weep!
But, for this woman,—if it so may be,—
Bid some Thessalian,—I entreat thee, king!—
Keep her,—who has not suffered like myself!
Many of the Pheraioi welcome thee.
Be no reminder to me of my ills!
I could not, if I saw her come to live,
Restrain the tear! Inflict on me, diseased,
No new disease: woe bends me down enough!
Then, where could she be sheltered in my house,
Female and young too? For that she is young,
The vesture and adornment prove. Reflect!
Should such an one inhabit the same roof
With men? And how, mixed up, a girl, with youths,
Shall she keep pure, in that case? No light task
To curb the May-day youngster, Herakles!
I only speak because of care for thee.

Or must I, in avoidance of such harm,
Make her to enter, lead her life within
The chamber of the dead one, all apart?
How shall I introduce this other, couch
This where Alkestis lay? A double blame
I apprehend: first, from the citizens—
Lest some tongue of them taunt that I betray
My benefactress, fall into the snare
Of a new fresh face: then, the dead one's self,—
Will she not blame me likewise? Worthy, sure,
Of worship from me! circumspect my ways,
And jealous of a fault, are bound to be.
But thou,—O woman, whosoe'er thou art,—
Know, thou hast all the form, art like as like
Alkestis, in the bodily shape! Ah me!
Take—by the Gods—this woman from my sight,
Lest thou undo me, the undone before!
Since I seem—seeing her—as if I saw
My own wife! And confusions cloud my heart,
And from my eyes the springs break forth! Ah me
Unhappy—how I taste for the first time
My misery in all its bitterness!"

Whereat the friends conferred: "The chance, in truth,
Was an untoward one—none said otherwise.
Still, what a God comes giving, good or bad,
That, one should take and bear with. Take her, then!"

Herakles,—not unfastening his hold
On that same misery, beyond mistake
Hoarse in the words, convulsive in the face,—
"I would that I had such a power," said he,
"As to lead up into the light again
Thy very wife, and grant thee such a grace!"

"Well do I know thou wouldst: but where the hope?
There is no bringing back the dead to light."

"Be not extravagant in grief, no less!
Bear it, by augury of better things!"

"'T is easier to advise 'bear up,' than bear!"

"But how carve way i' the life that lies before,
If bent on groaning ever for the past?"

"I myself know that: but a certain love
Allures me to the choice I shall not change."

"Ay, but, still loving dead ones, still makes weep."

"And let it be so! She has ruined me,
And still more than I say: that answers all."

"Oh, thou hast lost a brave wife: who disputes?"

"So brave a one—that he whom thou behold'st
Will never more enjoy his life again!"

"Time will assuage! The evil yet is young!"

"Time, thou mayst say, will; if time mean—to die."

"A wife—the longing for new marriage-joys
Will stop thy sorrow!"
                    "Hush, friend,—hold thy peace!
What hast thou said! I could not credit ear!"

"How then? Thou wilt not marry, then, but keep
A widowed couch?"
"There is not any one
Of womankind shall couch with whom thou seest!"

"Dost think to profit thus in any way
The dead one?"
                    "Her, wherever she abide,
My duty is to honor."
"And I praise—
Indeed I praise thee! Still, thou hast to pay
The price of it, in being held a fool!"

"Fool call me—only one name call me not!
Bridegroom!"
                    "No: it was praise, I portioned thee,
Of being good true husband to thy wife!"

"When I betray her, though she is no more,
May I die!"
                    And the thing he said was true:
For out of Herakles a great glow broke.
There stood a victor worthy of a prize:
The violet-crown that-withers on the brow
Of the half-hearted claimant. Oh, he knew
The signs of battle hard fought and well won,
This queller of the monsters!—knew his friend
Planted firm foot, now, on the loathly thing

That was Admetos late! "would die," he knew,
Ere let the reptile raise its crest again.
If that was truth, why try the true friend more?

"Then, since thou canst be faithful to the death,
Take, deep into thy house, my dame!" smiled he.

"Not so!—I pray, by thy Progenitor!"

"Thou wilt mistake in disobeying me!"

"Obeying thee, I have to break my heart!"

"Obey me! Who knows but the favor done
May fall into its place as duty too?"

So, he was humble, would decline no more
Bearing a burden: he just sighed, "Alas!
Would thou hadst never brought this prize from game!"

"Yet, when I conquered there, thou conqueredst!"

"All excellently urged! Yet—spite of all,
Bear with me! let the woman go away!"

"She shall go, if needs must: but ere she go,
See if there is need!"
                    "Need there is! At least,
Except I make thee angry with me, so!"

"But I persist, because I have my spice
Of intuition likewise: take the dame!"

"Be thou the victor, then! But certainly
Thou dost thy friend no pleasure in the act!"

"Oh, time will come when thou shalt praise me! Now—
Only obey!"
                    "Then, servants, since my house
Must needs receive this woman, take her there!"

"I shall not trust this woman to the care
Of servants."
                    "Why, conduct her in, thyself,
If that seem preferable!"
"I prefer,
With thy good leave, to place her in thy hands!"

"I would not touch her! Entry to the house—
That, I concede thee."
                    "To thy sole right hand
I mean to trust her!"
                    "King! Thou wrenchest this
Out of me by main force, if I submit!"

"Courage, friend! Come, stretch hand forth: Good! Now touch
The stranger-woman!"
                    "There! A hand I stretch—
As though it meant to cut off Gorgon's head!"

"Hast hold of her?"
                    "Fast hold."
                                "Why, then, hold fast
And have her! and, one day, asseverate
Thou wilt, I think, thy friend, the son of Zeus,
He was the gentle guest to entertain!
Look at her! See if she, in any way,
Present thee with resemblance of thy wife!"

Ah, but the tears come, find the words at fault!
There is no telling how the hero twitched
The veil off: and there stood, with such fixed eyes
And such slow smile, Alkestis' silent self!
It was the crowning grace of that great heart,
To keep back joy: procrastinate the truth
Until the wife, who had made proof and found
The husband wanting, might essay once more,
Hear, see, and feel him renovated now—
Able to do, now, all herself had done,
Risen to the height of her: so, hand in hand,
The two might go together, live and die.

Beside, when he found speech, you guess the speech.
He could not think he saw his wife again:
It was some mocking God that used the bliss
To make him mad! Till Herakles must help:
Assure him that no spectre mocked at all;
He was embracing whom he buried once.
Still,—did he touch, might he address the true,—
True eye, true body of the true live wife?

And Herakles said, smiling, "All was truth.
Spectre? Admetos had not made his guest
One who played ghost-invoker, or such cheat!
Oh, he might speak and have response, in time!
All heart could wish was gained now—life for death:

Only, the rapture must not grow immense:
Take care, nor wake the envy of the Gods!"

"O thou, of greatest Zeus true son,"—so spoke
Admetos when the closing word must come,
"Go ever in a glory of success,
And save, that sire, his offspring to the end!
For thou hast—only thou—raised me and mine
Up again to this light and life!" Then asked
Tremblingly, how was trod the perilous path
Out of the dark into the light and life:
How it had happened with Alkestis there.

And Herakles said little, but enough—
How he engaged in combat with that king
O' the dæmons: how the field of contest lay
By the tomb's self: how he sprang from ambuscade,
Captured Death, caught him in that pair of hands.

But all the time, Alkestis moved not once
Out of the set gaze and the silent smile;
And a cold fear ran through Admetos' frame:
"Why does she stand and front me, silent thus?"

Herakles solemnly replied, "Not yet
Is it allowable thou hear the things
She has to tell thee; let evanish quite
That consecration to the lower Gods,
And on our upper world the third day rise!
Lead her in, meanwhile; good and true thou art,
Good, true, remain thou! Practise piety
To stranger-guests the old way! So, farewell!
Since forth I fare, fulfil my urgent task
Set by the king, the son of Sthenelos."

Fain would Admetos keep that splendid smile
Ever to light him. "Stay with us, thou heart!
Remain our house-friend!"

                    "At some other day!
Now, of necessity, I haste!" smiled he.

"But mayst thou prosper, go forth on a foot
Sure to return! Through all the tetrarchy,
Command my subjects that they institute
Thanksgiving-dances for the glad event,
And bid each altar smoke with sacrifice!
For we are minded to begin a fresh

Existence, better than the life before;
Seeing I own myself supremely blest."

Whereupon all the friendly moralists
Drew this conclusion: chirped, each beard to each:
"Manifold are thy shapings, Providence!
Many a hopeless matter Gods arrange.
What we expected never came to pass:
What we did not expect Gods brought to bear;
So have things gone, this whole experience through!"

Ah, but if you had seen the play itself!
They say, my poet failed to get the prize:
Sophokles got the prize,—great name! They say,
Sophokles also means to make a piece,
Model a new Admetos, a new wife:
Success to him! One thing has many sides.
The great name! But no good supplants a good,
Nor beauty undoes beauty. Sophokles
Will carve and carry a fresh cup, brimful
Of beauty and good, firm to the altar-foot,
And glorify the Dionusiac shrine:
Not clash against this crater in the place
Where the God put it when his mouth had drained,
To the last dregs, libation lifeblood-like,
And praised Euripides forevermore—
The Human with his droppings of warm tears.

Still, since one thing may have so many sides,
I think I see how,—far from Sophokles,—
You, I, or any one might mould a new
Admetos, new Alkestis. Ah, that brave
Bounty of poets, the one royal race
That ever was, or will be, in this world!
They give no gift that hounds itself and ends
I' the giving and the taking: theirs so breeds
I' the heart and soul o' the taker, so transmutes
The man who only was a man before,
That he grows godlike in his turn, can give—
He also: share the poets' privilege,
Bring forth new good, new beauty, from the old.
As though the cup that gave the wine, gave, too,
The God's prolific giver of the grape,
That vine, was wont to find out, fawn around
His footstep, springing still to bless the dearth,
At bidding of a Mainad. So with me:
For I have drunk this poem, quenched my thirst,

Satisfied heart and soul—yet more remains!
Could we too make a poem? Try at least,
Inside the head, what shape the rose-mists take!

When God Apollon took, for punishment,
A mortal form and sold himself a slave
To King Admetos till a term should end,—
Not only did he make, in servitude,
Such music, while he fed the flocks and herds,
As saved the pasturage from wrong or fright,
Curing rough creatures of ungentleness:
Much more did that melodious wisdom work
Within the heart o' the master: there, ran wild
Many a lust and greed that grow to strength
By preying on the native pity and care,
Would else, all undisturbed, possess the land.

And these the God so tamed, with golden tongue,
That, in the plenitude of youth and power,
Admetos vowed himself to rule thenceforth
In Pherai solely for his people's sake,
Subduing to such end each lust and greed
That dominates the natural charity.

And so the struggle ended. Right ruled might:
And soft yet brave, and good yet wise, the man
Stood up to be a monarch; having learned
The worth of life, life's worth would he bestow
On all whose lot was cast, to live or die,
As he determined for the multitude.
So stands a statue: pedestalled sublime,
Only that it may wave the thunder off,
And ward, from winds that vex, a world below.

And then,—as if a whisper found its way
E'en to the sense o' the marble,—"Vain thy vow!
The royalty of its resolve, that head
Shall hide within the dust ere day be done:
That arm, its outstretch of beneficence,
Shall have a speedy ending on the earth:
Lie patient, prone, while light some cricket leaps
And takes possession of the masterpiece,
To sit, sing louder as more near the sun.
For why? A flaw was in the pedestal;
Who knows? A worm's work! Sapped, the certain fate
O' the statue is to fall, and thine to die!"

Whereat the monarch, calm, addressed himself

To die, but bitterly the soul outbroke—
"O prodigality of life, blind waste
I' the world, of power profuse without the will
To make life do its work, deserve its day!
My ancestors pursued their pleasure, poured
The blood o' the people out in idle war,
Or took occasion of some weary peace
To hid men dig down deep or build up high,
Spend bone and marrow that the king might feast
Entrenched and buttressed from the vulgar gaze.
Yet they all lived, nay, lingered to old age:
As though Zeus loved that they should laugh to scorn
The vanity of seeking other ends
In rule, than just the ruler's pastime. They
Lived; I must die."
                    And, as some long last moan
Of a minor suddenly is propped beneath
By note which, new-struck, turns the wail that was
Into a wonder and a triumph, so
Began Alkestis: "Nay, thou art to live!
The glory that, in the disguise of flesh,
Was helpful to our house,—he prophesied
The coming fate: whereon, I pleaded sore
That he,—I guessed a God, who to his couch
Amid the clouds must go and come again,
While we were darkling,—since he loved us both,
He should permit thee, at whatever price,
To live and carry out to heart's content
Soul's purpose, turn each thought to very deed,
Nor let Zeus lose the monarch meant in thee.

"To which Apollon, with a sunset smile,
Sadly—'and so should mortals arbitrate!
It were unseemly if they aped us Gods,
And, mindful of our chain of consequence,
Lost care of the immediate earthly link;
Forwent the comfort of life's little hour,
In prospect of some cold abysmal blank
Alien eternity,—unlike the time
They know, and understand to practise with,—
No,—our eternity—no heart's blood, bright
And warm outpoured in its behoof, would tinge
Never so palely, warm a whit the more:
Whereas retained and treasured—left to beat
Joyously on, a life's length, in the breast
O' the loved and loving—it would throb itself
Through, and suffuse the earthly tenement,
Transform it, even as your mansion here

Is love-transformed into a temple-home
Where I, a God, forget the Olumpian glow,
I' the feel of human richness like the rose:
Your hopes and fears, so blind and yet so sweet
With death about them. Therefore, well in thee
To look, not on eternity, but time:
To apprehend that, should Admetos die,
All, we Gods purposed in him, dies as sure:
That, life's link snapping, all our chain is lost.
And yet a mortal glance might pierce, methinks,
Deeper into the seeming dark of things,
And learn, no fruit, man's life can bear, will fade:
Learn, if Admetos die now, so much more
Will pity for the frailness found in flesh,
Will terror at the earthly chance and change
Frustrating wisest scheme of noblest soul,
Will these go wake the seeds of good asleep
Throughout the world: as oft a rough wind sheds
The unripe promise of some field-flower,—true!
But loosens too the level, and lets breathe
A thousand captives for the year to come.
Nevertheless, obtain thy prayer, stay fate!
Admetos lives—if thou wilt die for him!'

"So was the pact concluded that I die,
And thou live on, live for thyself, for me,
For all the world. Embrace and bid me hail,
Husband, because I have the victory—
Am, heart, soul, head to foot, one happiness!"

Whereto Admetos, in a passionate cry:
"Never, by that true word Apollon spoke!
All the unwise wish is unwished, O wife!
Let purposes of Zeus fulfil themselves,
If not through me, then through some other man!
Still, in myself he had a purpose too,
Inalienably mine, to end with me:
This purpose—that, throughout my earthly life,
Mine should be mingled and made up with thine,—
And we two prove one force and play one part
And do one thing. Since death divides the pair,
'T is well that I depart and thou remain
Who wast to me as spirit is to flesh:
Let the flesh perish, be perceived no more,
So thou, the spirit that informed the flesh,
Bend yet awhile, a very flame above
The rift I drop into the darkness by,—
And bid remember, flesh and spirit once

Worked in the world, one body, for man's sake.
Never be that abominable show
Of passive death without a quickening life—
Admetos only, no Alkestis now!"

Then she: "O thou Admetos, must the pile
Of truth on truth, which needs but one truth more
To tower up in completeness, trophy-like,
Emprise of man, and triumph of the world,
Must it go ever to the ground again
Because of some faint heart or faltering hand,
Which we, that breathless world about the base,
Trusted should carry safe to altitude,
Superimpose o' the summit, our supreme
Achievement, our victorious coping-stone?
Shall thine, Beloved, prove the hand and heart
That fail again, flinch backward at the truth
Would cap and crown the structure this last time,—
Precipitate our monumental hope
And strew the earth ignobly yet once more?
See how, truth piled on truth, the structure wants,
Waits justs the crowning truth I claim of thee!
Wouldst thou, for any joy to be enjoyed,
For any sorrow that thou mightst escape,
Unwill thy will to reign a righteous king?
Nowise! And were there two lots, death and life,—
Life, wherein good resolve should go to air,
Death, whereby finest fancy grew plain fact
I' the reign of thy survivor,—life or death?
Certainly death, thou choosest. Here stand I
The wedded, the beloved one: hadst thou loved
Her who less worthily could estimate
Both life and death than thou? Not so should say
Admetos, whom Apollon made come court
Alkestis in a car, submissive brutes
Of blood were yoked to, symbolizing soul
Must dominate unruly sense in man.
Then, shall Admetos and Alkestis see
Good alike, and alike choose, each for each,
Good,—and yet, each for other, at the last,
Choose evil? What? thou soundest in my soul
To depths below the deepest, reachest good
In evil, that makes evil good again,
And so allottest to me that I live
And not die—letting die, not thee alone,
But all true life that lived in both of us?
Look at me once ere thou decree the lot!"

Therewith her whole soul entered into his,
He looked the look back, and Alkestis died.

And even while it lay, i' the look of him,
Dead, the dimmed body, bright Alkestis' soul
Had penetrated through the populace
Of ghosts, was got to Koré,—throned and crowned
The pensive queen o' the twilight, where she dwells
Forever in a muse, but half away
From flowery earth she lost and hankers for,—
And there demanded to become a ghost
Before the time.
                    Whereat the softened eyes
Of the lost maidenhood that lingered still
Straying among the flowers in Sicily,
Sudden was startled back to Hades' throne
By that demand: broke through humanity
Into the orbed omniscience of a God,
Searched at a glance Alkestis to the soul,
And said—while a long slow sigh lost itself
I' the hard and hollow passage of a laugh:

"Hence, thou deceiver! This is not to die,
If, by the very death which mocks me now,
The life, that 's left behind and past my power,
Is formidably doubled. Say, there fight
Two athletes, side by side, each athlete armed
With only half the weapons, and no more,
Adequate to a contest with their foe:
If one of these should fling helm, sword and shield
To fellow—shieldless, swordless, helmless late—
And so leap naked o'er the barrier, leave
A combatant equipped from head to heel,
Yet cry to the other side, 'Receive a friend
Who fights no longer!' 'Back, friend, to the fray!'
Would be the prompt rebuff; I echo it.
Two souls in one were formidable odds:
Admetos must not be himself and thou!"

And so, before the embrace relaxed a whit,
The lost eyes opened, still beneath the look;
And lo, Alkestis was alive again,
And of Admetos' rapture who shall speak?

So, the two lived together long and well.
But never could I learn, by word of scribe
Or voice of poet, rumor wafts our way,
That—of the scheme of rule in righteousness,

The bringing back again the Golden Age,
Which, rather than renounce, our pair would die—
That ever one faint particle came true,
With both alive to bring it to effect:
Such is the envy Gods still bear mankind!

So might our version of the story prove,
And no Euripidean pathos plague
Too much my critic-friend of Syracuse.

"Besides your poem failed to get the prize:
(That is, the first prize: second prize is none.)
Sophokles got it!" Honor the great name!
All cannot love two great names; yet some do:
I know the poetess who graved in gold,
Among her glories that shall never fade,
This style and title for Euripides,
The Human with his droppings of warm tears.

I know, too, a great Kaunian painter, strong
As Herakles, though rosy with a robe
Of grace that softens down the sinewy strength:
And he has made a picture of it all.
There lies Alkestis dead, beneath the sun,
She longed to look her last upon, beside
The sea, which somehow tempts the life in us
To come trip over its white waste of waves,
And try escape from earth, and fleet as free.
Behind the body, I suppose there bends
Old Pheres in his hoary impotence;
And women-wailers in a corner crouch
—Four, beautiful as you four—yes, indeed!—
Close, each to other, agonizing all,
As fastened, in fear's rhythmic sympathy,
To two contending opposite. There strains
The might o' the hero 'gainst his more than match,
—Death, dreadful not in thew and bone, but like
The envenomed substance that exudes some dew
Whereby the merely honest flesh and blood
Will fester up and run to ruin straight,
Ere they can close with, clasp and overcome
The poisonous impalpability
That simulates a form beneath the flow
Of those gray garments; I pronounce that piece
Worthy to set up in our Poikilé!

And all came,—glory of the golden verse,
And passion of the picture, and that fine

Frank outgush of the human gratitude
Which saved our ship and me, in Syracuse,—
Ay, and the tear or two which slipt perhaps
Away from you, friends, while I told my tale,
—It all came of this play that gained no prize!
Why crown whom Zeus has crowned in soul before?

Robert Browning – A Short Biography

He is the equal of any Victorian Poet that could be mentioned. However, Browning continues to be in the shadow of Tennyson, Arnold, Hopkins, Morris and many others.

Robert Browning was born on May 7th, 1812 in Walworth in the parish of Camberwell, London. He was baptized on June 14th, 1812, at Lock's Fields Independent Chapel, York Street, Walworth.

Browning's early years were certainly very interesting. His mother was an excellent pianist and a very devout evangelical Christian. His father, who worked as a clerk at the Bank of England, was also an artist, scholar, antiquarian, and collector of books and pictures. Indeed, he amassed more than 6,000 volumes of rare books including works in Greek, Hebrew, Latin, French, Italian, and Spanish. For the young and curious Browning, it was a wonderful resource, added to which his father was a guiding force in his education.

Many accounts attest that Browning was already proficient at reading and writing by the age of five. He is said to have been a bright but anxious student and to have studied and learnt Latin, Greek, and French by the time he was fourteen. From fourteen to sixteen he was educated at home, tutored in music, drawing, dancing, and horsemanship. Certainly, language and the arts were two areas the young Browning both absorbed and pushed himself towards.

At the age of twelve he wrote a volume of Byronic verse he called Incondita, which his parents attempted to have published. The attempts were unsuccessful and, disappointed, Browning destroyed the work.

In 1825, a cousin gave Browning a collection of Percy Bysshe Shelley's poetry; Browning was so enamored with the poems that he asked for the rest of Shelley's works for his thirteenth birthday. In fact, Browning then went the extra mile, declaring himself to be both a vegetarian and an atheist in honour of his hero.

Intriguingly it seems that the rejection of his first volume didn't dim his appreciation of other poets, but it appears to have stopped him writing any poems between the ages of thirteen and twenty.

In 1828, Browning enrolled at the newly-opened University of London. He was uncomfortable with the experience and he soon left, anxious to read and absorb at his own pace.

His education which, overall is notably rambling and lacks a structure that many of his artistic contemporaries enjoyed, i.e. excellent public schooling and then a degree at Oxford or Cambridge, may present many of his critics with ammunition to criticize, but alternatively his hap-hazard education certainly contributed to many of the references that baffled both critics and his audience, but they tellingly show the breath and scale of what he could turn words too. What others would call obscure references were, to Browning, remarkably obvious.

Browning's early career was very promising. His long poem Pauline (of which only a fragment was ever finished and published) brought him to the attention of the Pre-Raphaelite master Dante Gabriel Rossetti and his difficult Paracelsus (published in 1835) was warmly admired by both Dickens and Wordsworth.

In the 1830s he met the actor William Macready and was encouraged to develop and turn his talents to the stage by writing verse drama. But these plays, including Strafford, which ran for five nights in 1837, and those contained within the Bells and Pomegranates series, were, for the most part, unsuccessful.

During this period Browning began to discover that his real talents lay in taking a single character and allowing that character to discover more about himself by revealing further personal aspects of himself in his speeches; the dramatic monologue. The techniques he developed through this—especially the use of diction, rhythm, and symbol—are regarded as his most important contribution to poetry. They would later influence such major poets of the 20th Century as Ezra Pound, T. S. Eliot, and Robert Frost.

By 1840, with the publication of Sordello, the tide turned somewhat. Many thought he was being deliberately obscure, opaque beyond measure and his poetry for the next decade or so was not eagerly acquired or talked about.

As Browning attempted to rehabilitate his career he began a relationship with Elizabeth Barrett in 1845. He had read her poems and, being totally charmed by their quality, was determined to meet her. The poetess was better known than the younger Browning but suffered from a debilitating illness and was also subject to the harsh behaviour of her over-bearing father. Nevertheless, the new couple were soon inseparable.

Her father, as he did with any of his children that married, disinherited her. Despite this she had some money from her own resources and sensing that the best outcome for both the relationship and her own health was to move abroad the couple did just that. After a private marriage at St Marylebone Parish Church, in September 1846, they journeyed to Europe to honeymoon in Paris.

Their new life now took them to Italy, first to Pisa and a little later to Florence. There they absorbed life and one another.

But in the short term the literary assault on Browning's work did not let up. He was now criticized by such patrician writers as Charles Kingsley for his abandonment of England for foreign lands. Browning could do little to answer these attacks except to compose with his pen and continue with his poetical journey.

The Browning's were well respected, and even famous. Elizabeth health began to improve, she grew stronger and in 1849, at the age of 43, between four miscarriages, she gave birth to a son, Robert Wiedeman Barrett Browning, whom they nicknamed "Penini" or "Pen",

Intriguingly despite his growing reputation and return to form as a poet he was more often than not known as 'Elizabeth Barrett's husband'.

Work flowed from his pen that was to ensure his reputation as one of England's leading poets. When his collection Men and Women was published in 1855 it contained some of his finest lines. It was dedicated to Elizabeth. Life had begun to smile handsome rewards upon the Brownings.

Victorian society was very much taken with all things spiritualist. It was not enough to have command of much of the globe through Empire, they wished to know and explore wherever they could. The spirit world beckoned their interest. Browning dissented from this view believing it was all a hoax and a fraud. Elizabeth, however, was inclined to believe and this caused several disagreements between the couple.

They attended a séance by Daniel Dunglas Home, in July 1855. (Home was a famous and clamored after Scottish physical medium with the reported ability to levitate and speak with the dead). It is said that during this séance a spirit face materialised. Home then claimed it was the face of Browning's son who had died in infancy. Browning seized the 'materialisation' which turned out to be Home's bare foot. Browning had never lost a son in infancy.

After the séance, Browning wrote an angry letter to The Times, in which he said: "the whole display of hands, spirit utterances etc., was a cheat and imposture."

The Browning's time in Italy were immensely rewarding years for both their personal and professional lives. Browning encouraged her to include Sonnets from the Portuguese in her published works, these beautiful poems are undoubtedly one of the highlights of English love poetry.

Elizabeth had become quite politicised during these years. Engrossed in Italian politics (which was continuing to slowly re-unify the country), she issued a small volume of political poems entitled Poems before Congress (1860) most of which were written to express her sympathy with the Italian cause after the earlier outbreak of The Second Italian Independence War in 1859. In England they caused uproar. Conservative magazines such as Blackwood's and the Saturday Review labelled her a fanatic. She dedicated the book to her husband.

But in 1861 tragedy struck.

The couple had spent the winter of 1860–61 in Rome when Elizabeth's health deteriorated again and they returned to Florence in early June. However, these turned out to be her final weeks. Only morphine would now still the pain. She died in Browning's arms on June 29th, 1861. Browning said that she died "smilingly, happily, and with a face like a girl's .... Her last word was .... ''Beautiful".

Her burial took place in the nearby Protestant English Cemetery of Florence. The local people were deeply saddened, and shops closed their doors in grief and respect.

Browning and their son were obviously devastated. Unable to bear being in Florence without Elizabeth they soon returned to London to live at 19 Warwick Crescent, Maida Vale.

As he re-integrated himself back into the London literary scene he began to finally receive the proper praise, respect and reputation that his works deserved.

Browning went on to publish Dramatis Personæ (1864), and The Ring and the Book (1868–1869). The latter, based on an "old yellow book" which told of a seventeenth-century Italian murder trial, received wide and generous critical acclaim. Although by now he was in the twilight of a long and prolific career, that had achieved some notable ups and downs, he was respected and indeed renowned for his talents and works.

In 1878, he revisited Italy for the first time since Elizabeth's death. He would return there on several further occasions but never to Florence.

Such was the esteem he was held in that The Browning Society was founded in 1881. Although he had never obtained a degree (something that set him apart from many other Victorian poets) he was now awarded honorary degrees from Oxford University in 1882 and then the University of Edinburgh in 1884.

In 1887, Browning produced the major work of his later years, Parleyings with Certain People of Importance in Their Day. Browning now spoke with his own voice as he engaged in a series of dialogues with long-forgotten figures of literary, artistic, and philosophic history. Unfortunately, both the critics and public were completely baffled by this.

On April 7th, 1889 Browning attended a dinner party at the home of his friend, the artist Rudolf Lehmann. The highlight of which was a recording made on a wax cylinder on an Edison cylinder phonograph. On the recording, which still exists, Browning recites part of How They Brought the Good News from Ghent to Aix, and can even be heard apologising when he forgets the words.

The recording was first played in 1890 on the anniversary of his death, at a gathering of his admirers, it was said to be the first time anyone's voice 'had been heard from beyond the grave'.

His last work Asolando: Fancies and Facts (1889), returned to his brief and concise lyric verse that was so popular. It was published on the day of his death on December 12th, 1889, Robert Browning was at his son's home Ca' Rezzonico in Venice.

He was buried in Poets' Corner in Westminster Abbey; his grave lies immediately adjacent to that of Alfred Tennyson.

Among the many who have publicly acknowledged their literary debt to him are Henry James, Oscar Wilde, George Bernard Shaw, G. K. Chesterton, Ezra Pound, Jorge Luis Borges, and Vladimir Nabokov.

Robert Browning - A Concise Bibliography

Here follows a list of the plays and poetry volumes published during his lifetime. Poems of particular worth are noted from within those volumes.

Pauline: A Fragment of a Confession (1833)
Paracelsus (1835)
Strafford (play) (1837)
Sordello (1840)
Bells and Pomegranates No. I: Pippa Passes (play) (1841)
        The Year's at the Spring
Bells and Pomegranates No. II: King Victor and King Charles (play) (1842)

Bells and Pomegranates No. III: Dramatic Lyrics (1842)
> *Porphyria's Lover*
> *Soliloquy of the Spanish Cloister*
> *My Last Duchess*
> *The Pied Piper of Hamelin*
> *Count Gismond*
> *Johannes Agricola in Meditation*

Bells and Pomegranates No. IV: The Return of the Druses (play) (1843)
Bells and Pomegranates No. V: A Blot in the 'Scutcheon (play) (1843)
Bells and Pomegranates No. VI: Colombe's Birthday (play) (1844)
Bells and Pomegranates No. VII: Dramatic Romances and Lyrics (1845)
> *The Laboratory*
> *How They Brought the Good News from Ghent to Aix*
> *The Bishop Orders His Tomb at Saint Praxed's Church*
> *The Lost Leader*
> *Home Thoughts from Abroad*
> *Meeting at Night*

Bells and Pomegranates No. VIII: Luria and A Soul's Tragedy (plays) (1846)
Christmas-Eve and Easter-Day (1850)
An Essay on Percy Bysshe Shelley (essay) (1852)
Two Poems (1854)
Men and Women (1855)
> *Love Among the Ruins*
> *A Toccata of Galuppi's*
> *Childe Roland to the Dark Tower Came*
> *Fra Lippo Lippi*
> *Andrea Del Sarto*
> *The Patriot*
> *The Last Ride Together*
> *Memorabilia*
> *Cleon*
> *How It Strikes a Contemporary*
> *The Statue and the Bust*
> *A Grammarian's Funeral*
> *An Epistle Containing the Strange Medical Experience of Karshish, the Arab Physician*
> *Bishop Blougram's Apology*
> *Master Hugues of Saxe-Gotha*
> *By the Fire-side*

Dramatis Personae (1864)
> *Caliban upon Setebos*
> *Rabbi Ben Ezra*
> *Abt Vogler*
> *Mr. Sludge, "The Medium"*
> *Prospice*
> *A Death in the Desert*

The Ring and the Book (1868–69)
Balaustion's Adventure (1871)
Prince Hohenstiel-Schwangau, Saviour of Society (1871)

Fifine at the Fair (1872)
Red Cotton Night-Cap Country, or, Turf and Towers (1873)
Aristophanes' Apology (1875)
    Thamuris Marching
The Inn Album (1875)
Pacchiarotto, and How He Worked in Distemper (1876)
    Numpholeptos
The Agamemnon of Aeschylus (1877)
La Saisiaz and The Two Poets of Croisic (1878)
Dramatic Idylls (1879)
Dramatic Idylls: Second Series (1880)
    Pan and Luna
Jocoseria (1883)
Ferishtah's Fancies (1884)
Parleyings with Certain People of Importance in Their Day (1887)
Asolando (1889)
    Prologue
    Summum Bonum
    Bad Dreams III
    Flute-Music, with an Accompaniment
    Epilogue